Great COUNTRY HITS of the 90s

60 Great Songs for EZ GUITAR

DON'T TAKE THE GIR

Recorded by Tim McGraw on Curb Records
Words and Music by Craig Martin and Larry W. Johnson

I'LL TRY

Recorded by ALAN JACKSON

LET ME LET GO

Recorded by FAITH HILL (with VINCE GILL) on Warner Bros. Records

Words and Music by DENNIS MORGAN and STEVE DIAMOND

Two Teardrops

Project Managers: Aaron Stang & Colgan Bryan
Music Editor: Colgan Bryan
Art Design: Design O'Rama

CONTENTS

ANY MAN OF MINE .... Shania Twain 6
A BAD GOODBYE .... Clint Black/Wynonna 10
BREATHE .... Faith Hill 12
BURNIN' THE ROADHOUSE DOWN .... Steve Wariner 15
BUTTERFLY KISSES .... Bob Carlisle 18
CHATTAHOOCHIE .... Alan Jackson 22
CONSTANT CRAVING .... K.D. Lang 24
THE DANCE .... Garth Brooks 26
DID I SHAVE MY LEGS FOR THIS? .... Deanna Carter 28
DON'T FENCE ME IN .... Lari White 87
DON'T ROCK THE JUKEBOX .... Alan Jackson 30
DON'T TAKE THE GIRL .... Tim McGraw 32
FAST AS YOU .... Dwight Yoakam 34
FEELS LIKE HOME .... LeAnn Rimes 36
FOR YOU I WILL .... Aaron Tippin 42
FOREVER'S AS FAR AS I'LL GO .... Alabama 44
FROM THIS MOMENT ON .... Shania Twain 39
GO REST HIGH ON THAT MOUNTAIN .... Vince Gill 46
GOD BLESS TEXAS .... Little Texas 50
GONE COUNTRY .... Alan Jackson 47
HOLES IN THE FLOOR OF HEAVEN .... Steve Wariner 52
HONEY I'M HOME .... Shania Twain 54
HOW DO I LIVE .... LeAnn Rimes 60
I CAN LOVE YOU LIKE THAT .... John Michael Montgomery 62
I CAN STILL FEEL YOU .... Collin Raye 57
I DON'T EVEN KNOW HER NAME .... Alan Jackson 64
I DON'T WANT TO MISS A THING .... Mark Chesnutt 67
I STILL BELIEVE IN YOU .... Vince Gill 70
I SWEAR .... John Michael Montgomery 72
I WILL ALWAYS LOVE YOU .... Dolly Parton 74
IF YOU EVER HAVE FOREVER IN MIND .... Vince Gill 78

I'LL TRY	Alan Jackson	76
IN ANOTHER'S EYES	Trisha Yearwood & Garth Brooks	80
IN THIS LIFE	Collin Raye	82
INDIAN OUTLAW	Tim McGraw	84
JUST TO HEAR YOU SAY THAT YOU LOVE ME	Faith Hill with Tim McGraw	90
KICK A LITTLE	Little Texas	92
LET ME LET GO	Faith Hill	94
LIFE GOES ON	Little Texas	97
LONG NECK BOTTLE	Garth Brooks	100
LOOKING THROUGH YOUR EYES	LeAnn Rimes	102
LOOSEN UP MY STRINGS	Clint Black	105
MERCURY BLUES	Alan Jackson	108
NEVER KNEW LONELY	Vince Gill	110
POOR, POOR PITIFUL ME	Terri Clark	112
THE RIVER	Garth Brooks	115
SHE'S GONNA MAKE IT	Garth Brooks	118
SOMEONE YOU USED TO KNOW	Collin Raye	120
SOMETHING THAT WE DO	Clint Black	122
THAT DON'T IMPRESS ME MUCH	Shania Twain	126
THIS KISS	Faith Hill	132
TWO TEARDROPS	Steve Wariner	129
WHAT IF JESUS COMES BACK LIKE THAT	Collin Raye	134
WHAT THE COWGIRLS DO	Vince Gill	136
WHERE THE GREEN GRASS GROWS	Tim McGraw	138
WRONG NIGHT	Reba McEntire	140
YOU BETTER THINK TWICE	Vince Gill	146
YOU MOVE ME	Garth Brooks	143
YOU'RE EASY ON THE EYES	Terri Clark	150
YOU'RE STILL THE ONE	Shania Twain	148

ARTIST INDEX

Alabama

FOREVER'S AS FAR AS I'LL GO 44

Clint Black

LOOSEN UP MY STRINGS 105
SOMETHING THAT WE DO 122

Clint Black/Wynonna

A BAD GOODBYE 10

Garth Brooks

THE DANCE 26
LONG NECK BOTTLE 100
THE RIVER 115
SHE'S GONNA MAKE IT 118
YOU MOVE ME 143

Bob Carlisle

BUTTERFLY KISSES 18

Deana Carter

DID I SHAVE MY LEGS FOR THIS? 28

Mark Chesnutt

I DON'T WANT TO MISS A THING 67

Terri Clark

POOR, POOR PITIFUL ME 112
YOU'RE EASY ON THE EYES 150

Vince Gill

GO REST HIGH ON THAT MOUNTAIN 46
I STILL BELIEVE IN YOU 70
IF YOU EVER HAVE FOREVER IN MIND 78
NEVER KNEW LONELY 110
WHAT THE COWGIRLS DO 136
YOU BETTER THINK TWICE 146

Faith Hill

BREATHE 12
LET ME LET GO 94
THIS KISS 132

Faith Hill with Tim McGraw

JUST TO HEAR YOU SAY THAT YOU LOVE ME 90

Alan Jackson

CHATTAHOOCHIE 22
DON'T ROCK THE JUKEBOX 30
GONE COUNTRY 47
I DON'T EVEN KNOW HER NAME 64
I'LL TRY 76
MERCURY BLUES 108

K.D. Lang

CONSTANT CRAVING 24

Little Texas

GOD BLESS TEXAS 50
KICK A LITTLE 92
LIFE GOES ON 97

Reba McEntire

WRONG NIGHT 140

Tim McGraw

DON'T TAKE THE GIRL 32
INDIAN OUTLAW 84
WHERE THE GREEN GRASS GROWS 138

John Michael Montgomery

I CAN LOVE YOU LIKE THAT 62
I SWEAR 72

Dolly Parton

I WILL ALWAYS LOVE YOU 74

Collin Raye

I CAN STILL FEEL YOU 57
IN THIS LIFE 82
SOMEONE YOU USED TO KNOW 120
WHAT IF JESUS COMES BACK LIKE THAT 134

LeAnn Rimes

FEELS LIKE HOME 36
HOW DO I LIVE 60
LOOKING THROUGH YOUR EYES 102

Aaron Tippin

FOR YOU I WILL 42

Shania Twain

ANY MAN OF MINE 6
FROM THIS MOMENT ON 39
HONEY I'M HOME 54
THAT DON'T IMPRESS ME MUCH 126
YOU'RE STILL THE ONE 148

Steve Wariner

BURNIN' THE ROADHOUSE DOWN 15
HOLES IN THE FLOOR OF HEAVEN 52
TWO TEARDROPS 129

Lari White

DON'T FENCE ME IN 87

Trisha Yearwood & Garth Brooks

IN ANOTHER'S EYES 80

Dwight Yoakam

FAST AS YOU 34

ANY MAN OF MINE

Words and Music by
SHANIA TWAIN and R. J. LANGE

C5 D♭5
mil - lion times, I wan - na hear him say,
E♭5
"Yeah, yeah, yeah, yeah, yeah, I like it that
Country two-beat
Chorus:
D♭
way!" An - y man of mine
A♭
bet - ter walk the line. Bet - ter show me a
E♭ A♭
teas - in', squeez - in', pleas - in' kind of time.
D♭
I need a man who knows how the sto - ry
A♭ G♭
goes. He's got - ta be a heart - beat - in', fine treat - in',
D♭ E♭
breath - tak - in', earth - quak - in' kind,

1.
N.C.
A♭5
any man of mine.
E♭5
A♭5
3. And
2.
N.C.
any man of
D♭
mine.
(Instrumental solo . . .
A♭
D♭
. . . end solo) Let me hear you say,
E♭
"Yeah, yeah, yeah, yeah,
yeah, I like it that
E♭7
way!"
A♭
Any man, any
man, any man...
Chorus:
B♭7
Any man of
E♭
mine
better walk the
B♭
line.
Better show me a
F
teas-in', squeez-in', pleas-in' kind of
B♭
time.

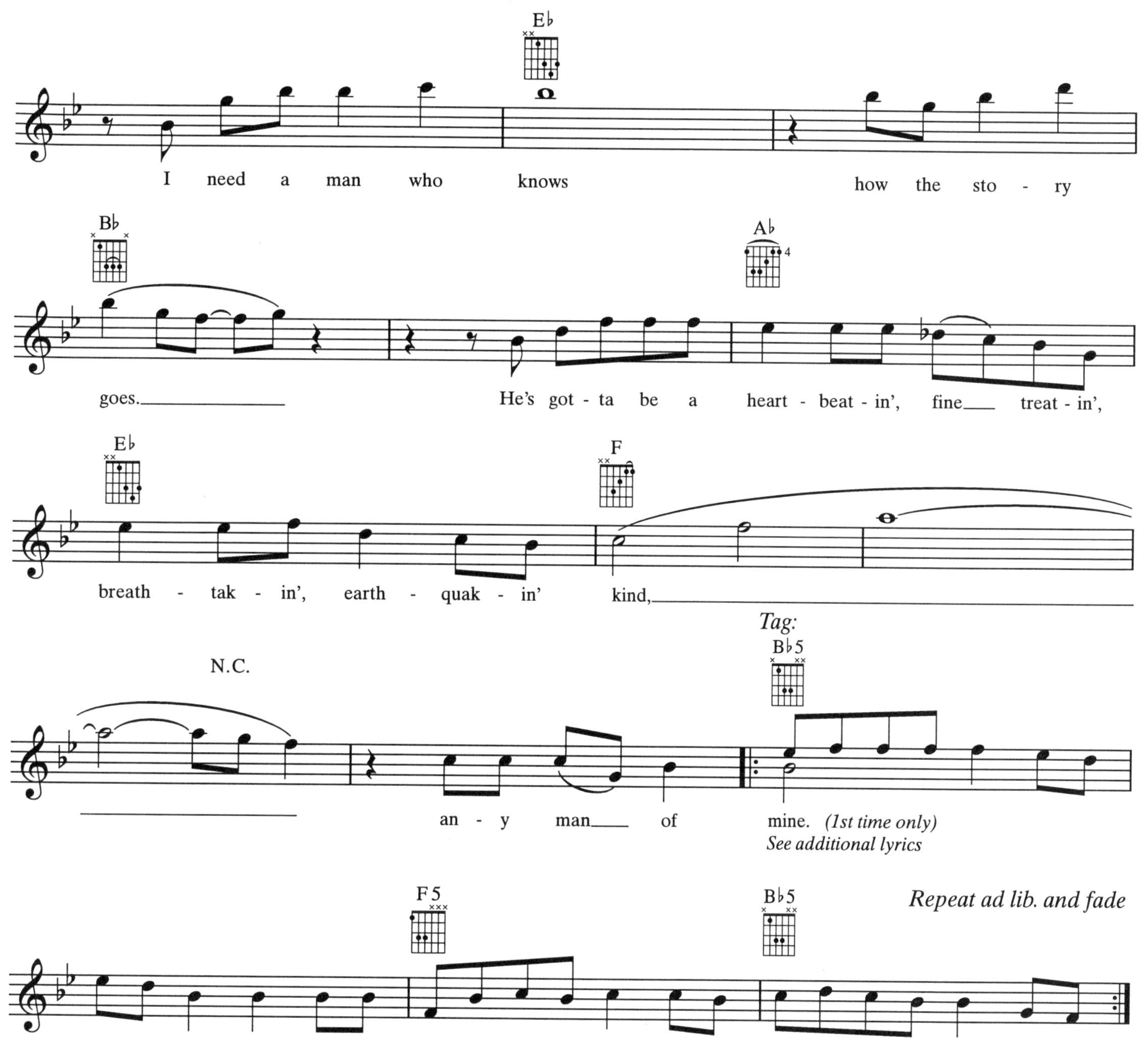

Tag:
You gotta shimmy shake, make the earth quake.
Kick, turn, stomp, stomp, then you jump heel to toe, Do Si Do
'Til your boots wanna break, 'til your feet and your back ache,
Keep it movin' 'til you just can't take anymore.
Come on, everybody on the floor, a-one two, a-three four.
Hup two, hup if you wanna be a man of mine, that's right.
This is what a woman wants...

A BAD GOODBYE

Words and Music by
CLINT BLACK

To Coda ⊕ *Verse 2:*

F/G G C F/C

find - ing none. I'm still bound to leave_ you.

Em7 F Am

I sure - ly don't know_ how. My heart won't let me

D7 Dm7 G

put_ you through_ what my mind_ said should have been hell._

C F/C Am

I don't know where we'll go_ from here,_ there may be_ no way to_

D7 Dm7 Am7

fly._ And the cloud I'm in just_ makes it all_ too_ clear that I can't_

Dm7 G G7 C *D.S.* 𝄋 *al Coda*

leave_ you with_ a bad_ good - bye. Good -

⊕ *Coda*

C F/C Am

How can we be so far_ be - tween_ where we are and one more_

D7 Dm7 Am7

try?_ And an - y way I_ look, I've on - ly_ seen that I can't_

Dm7 G7 C Dm/C C

leave_ you with_ a bad_ good - bye. *rit.*

BREATHE

Words and Music by
HOLLY LAMAR and STEPHANIE BENTLEY

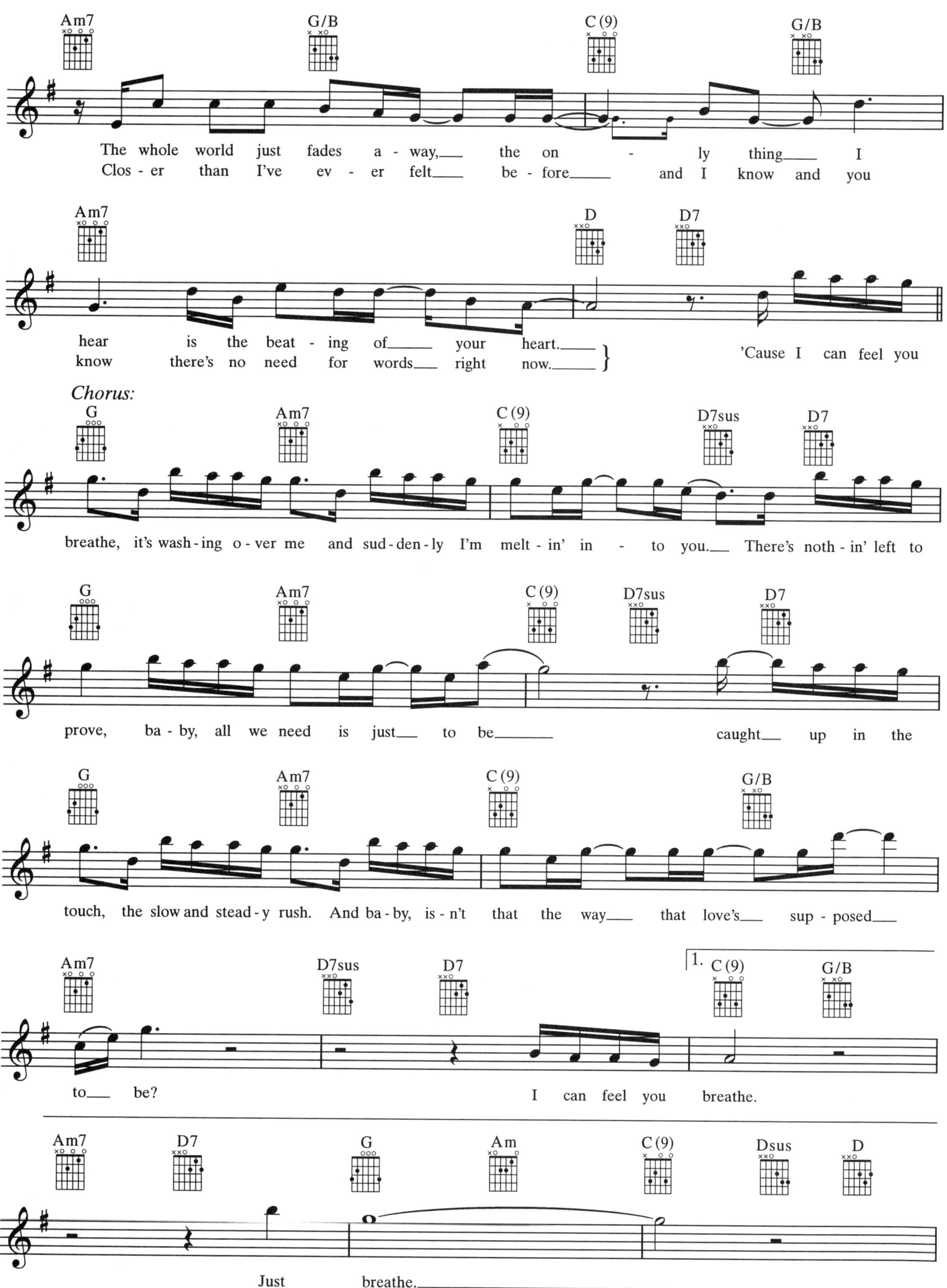
Am7
G/B
C (9)
G/B
The whole world just fades a - way, the on - ly thing I
Clos - er than I've ev - er felt be - fore and I know and you
Am7
D
D7
hear is the beat - ing of your heart.
know there's no need for words right now.
'Cause I can feel you
Chorus:
G
Am7
C (9)
D7sus
D7
breathe, it's wash - ing o - ver me and sud - den - ly I'm melt - in' in - to you. There's noth - in' left to
G
Am7
C (9)
D7sus
D7
prove, ba - by, all we need is just to be caught up in the
G
Am7
C (9)
G/B
touch, the slow and stead - y rush. And ba - by, is - n't that the way that love's sup - posed
Am7
D7sus
D7
1. C (9)
G/B
to be? I can feel you breathe.
Am7
D7
G
Am
C (9)
Dsus
D
Just breathe.

G Am C (9) Dsus
2.
C (9) G/B
breathe.
Am7 Dsus G Am7 C (9) Dsus D G Am7
Just breathe.
C (9) D7sus G Am7
Caught up in the touch, the slow and stead - y rush. And ba - by, is - n't
C (9) G/B Am7
that the way that love's sup - posed to be?
D7sus D7 C (9) G/B Am7 D7sus
I can feel you breathe. Just
G Am7 C (9) G/B Am7 G/B
breathe. I can feel the mag - ic float - ing in
C (9) G/B Am7 G/B C (9)
the air; be - ing with you gets me that way.
rit.

BURNIN' THE ROADHOUSE DOWN

Words and Music by
RICK CARNES and STEVE WARINER

C dim7
A/C♯
D7
down. The band___ is in___ full swing___ and man, there ain't___
B9
E7
A6
___ no stop - pin' now.___ There'll be noth - in' left___ but ash -
A7
D7
- es___ when Sun - day rolls a - round,___ but
To Coda
A6
F♯7
B9
E7
it's al - right,___ it's Sat - ur - day night___ and we're burn - in' the road - house
Guitar Solo:
A6
A6
A7
down.
D7
A6
F♯7
B9
E7

A6
A7
D7
A6
F♯7
B7
E7
A6
D.S. 𝄋 al Coda
2. Yeah, it's a mob
Coda
A6
down. They'll be sift - in' through the ash -
A7
D7
E♭dim7
- es when Sun - day rolls a - round, but
A6
A7
F♯7
B9
E7
it's al - right, it's Sat - ur - day night and we're burn - in' the road - house
A6
down.
D7
A6
A♭
F♯7
F♯
B9
F7
E7
A6

BUTTERFLY KISSES

Words and Music by
BOB CARLISLE and RANDY THOMAS

Gsus
oh, but most of all, for
she leaned o - ver, and gave me
Chorus:
Csus2 sus4
C
but - ter - fly kiss - es af - ter bed - time prayer, stick - in'
but - ter - fly kiss - es with her ma - ma there, stick - in'
G/C
3fr.
Am
G
lit - tle white flow - ers all up in her hair.
lit - tle white flow - ers all up in her hair.
F(9)
C/E
Cont. rhy. simile
"Walk be - side the po - ny, dad - dy, it's my first ride." "I
"Walk me down the aisle, dad - dy, it's just a - bout time." "Does my
know the cake looks fun - ny, dad - dy, but I sure tried." Oh, with
wed - ding gown look pret - ty, dad - dy?" "Dad - dy, don't cry." Oh, with
F/A
G/B
Dsus
D
To Coda
all that I've done wrong, I must have done some-thing right to de - serve a
all that I've done wrong, I must have done some-thing right to de - serve her
G7sus
hug ev - 'ry morn - ing and but - ter - fly kiss - es at night.
Asus2 sus4
F/G
C(9)

Verse 2:
Am C Am
Sweet six - teen to - day; she's look - ing like her ma - ma a lit - tle
C Dm7 C/E F6 Gsus G
more ev - 'ry day. One part wom - an, the oth - er part girl; to
Dm7 C/E F(9) Gsus G F/A G/B
per - fume and make - up from rib - bons and curls; try - ing her wings out in a
C(9) F(9)/A Gsus
great big world. But I re - mem - ber
Chorus:
Csus2 sus4 C Csus2 sus4 C Csus2 sus4 C
but - ter - fly kiss - es af - ter bed - time prayer, stick - in' lit - tle white flow - ers all
G/C 3fr. Asus2 sus4 G F(9)
Cont. rhy. simile
up in her hair. "You know how much I love you, dad - dy, but if
C/E F(9)
you don't mind, I'm on - ly gon - na kiss you on the cheek
C/E F/A G/B
this time." Oh, with all that I've done wrong, I must have done

C Dsus D F(9)

some - thing right ___ to de - serve her love ev - 'ry morn - ing and

G7sus Csus2 sus4 C Csus2 sus4 C

but - ter - fly kiss - es at night. ___ (All the pre - cious

Bridge:

E♭ Dm Csus2 sus4 C Csus2 sus4 C

time. ___) Oh, like the wind, the years _ go ___ by. ___ (Pre - cious but - ter -

E♭ Dm7 F/A G *D.S. 𝄋 al Coda*

fly, ___ spread your wings and fly.)

𝄌 *Coda*

F(9) G7sus F/A

love ev - 'ry morn - ing and but - ter - fly kiss - es. ___ I could - n't ask God _ for more, _ man,

G/B A♭maj9 C/G *poco rit.*

this is what love is. ___ I know I've got _ to let _ her go, but I'll al - ways ___ re - mem - ber ___

Freely

F(9) Gsus

___ ev - 'ry hug in the morn - ing and but - ter - fly kiss - es. ___

Csus2 sus4 C Csus2 sus4 C Csus2 sus4 C G/A G7sus C

a tempo *rit.*

CHATTAHOOCHEE

Words and Music by
ALAN JACKSON and JIM McBRIDE

Verse 2:
Well, we fogged up the windows in my old Chevy,
I was willin', but she wasn't ready.
So I settled for a burger and a grape sno-cone.
I dropped her off early, but I didn't go home.
(To Chorus:)

CONSTANT CRAVING

Words and Music by
k.d. lang and BEN MINK

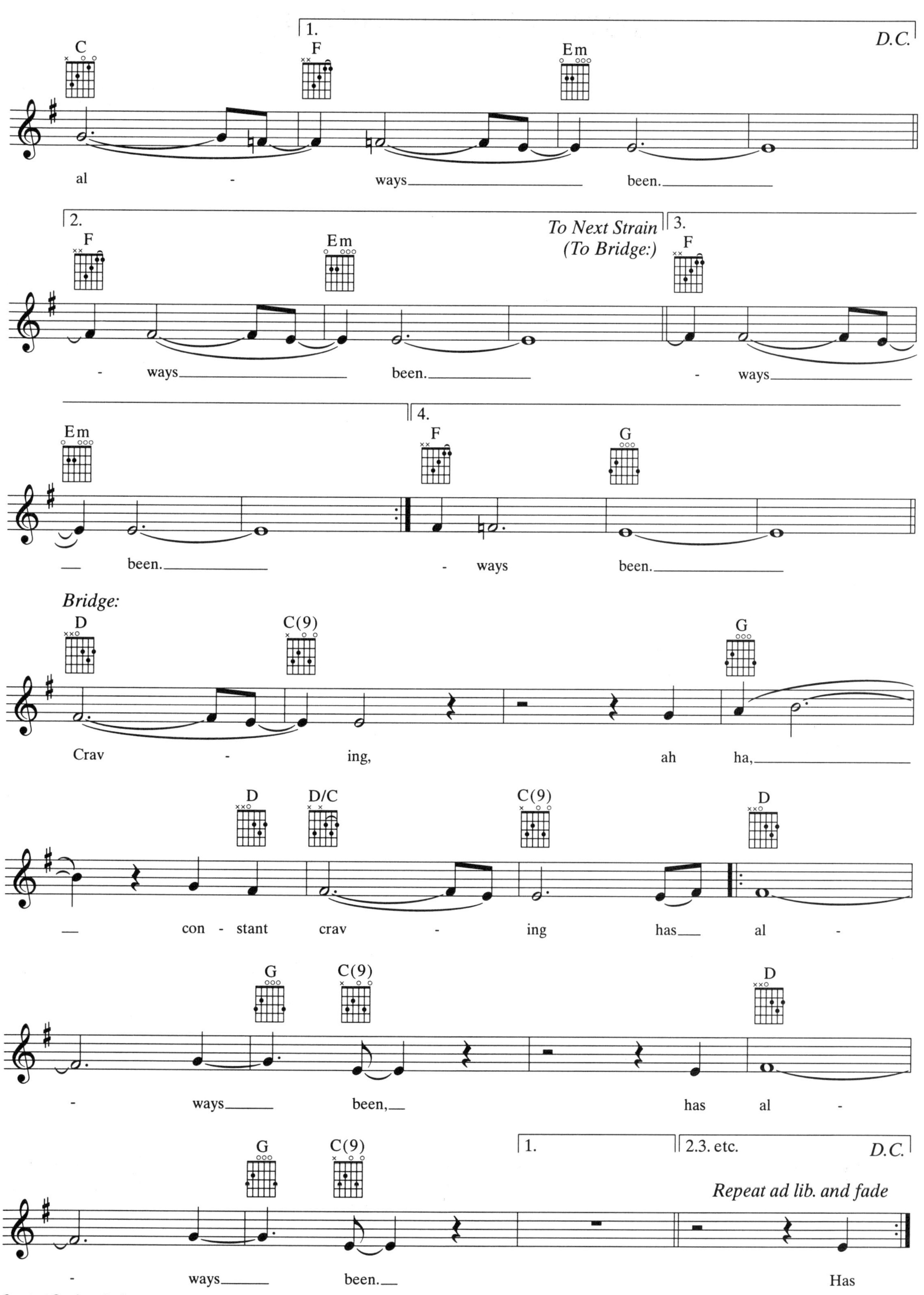
1.
D.C.
C
F
Em
al - ways been.
2.
F
Em
To Next Strain
(To Bridge:)
3.
F
- ways been. - ways
Em
4.
F
G
been. - ways been.
Bridge:
D
C(9)
G
Crav - ing, ah ha,
D
D/C
C(9)
D
con - stant crav - ing has al -
G
C(9)
D
- ways been, has al -
G
C(9)
1.
2.3. etc.
D.C.
Repeat ad lib. and fade
- ways been. Has

THE DANCE

Words and Music by
TONY ARATA

C
D
are bet - ter left to chance. I could have missed the pain,
Bm7
C
D
but I'd have had to miss the
1.
G
C/G
G
C/G
G
D
C
G
dance.
2. Hold - ing you
2.
G
C
dance. Yes, my life, it's bet - ter left to chance
D
Bm7
I could have missed the pain, but I'd have had to miss
C
D
N.C.
Em
the dance.
C
D
Em
Repeat ad lib. and fade
C
Dsus
D
Em

DID I SHAVE MY LEGS FOR THIS?

Words and Music by
DEANA KAY CARTER and RHONDA HART

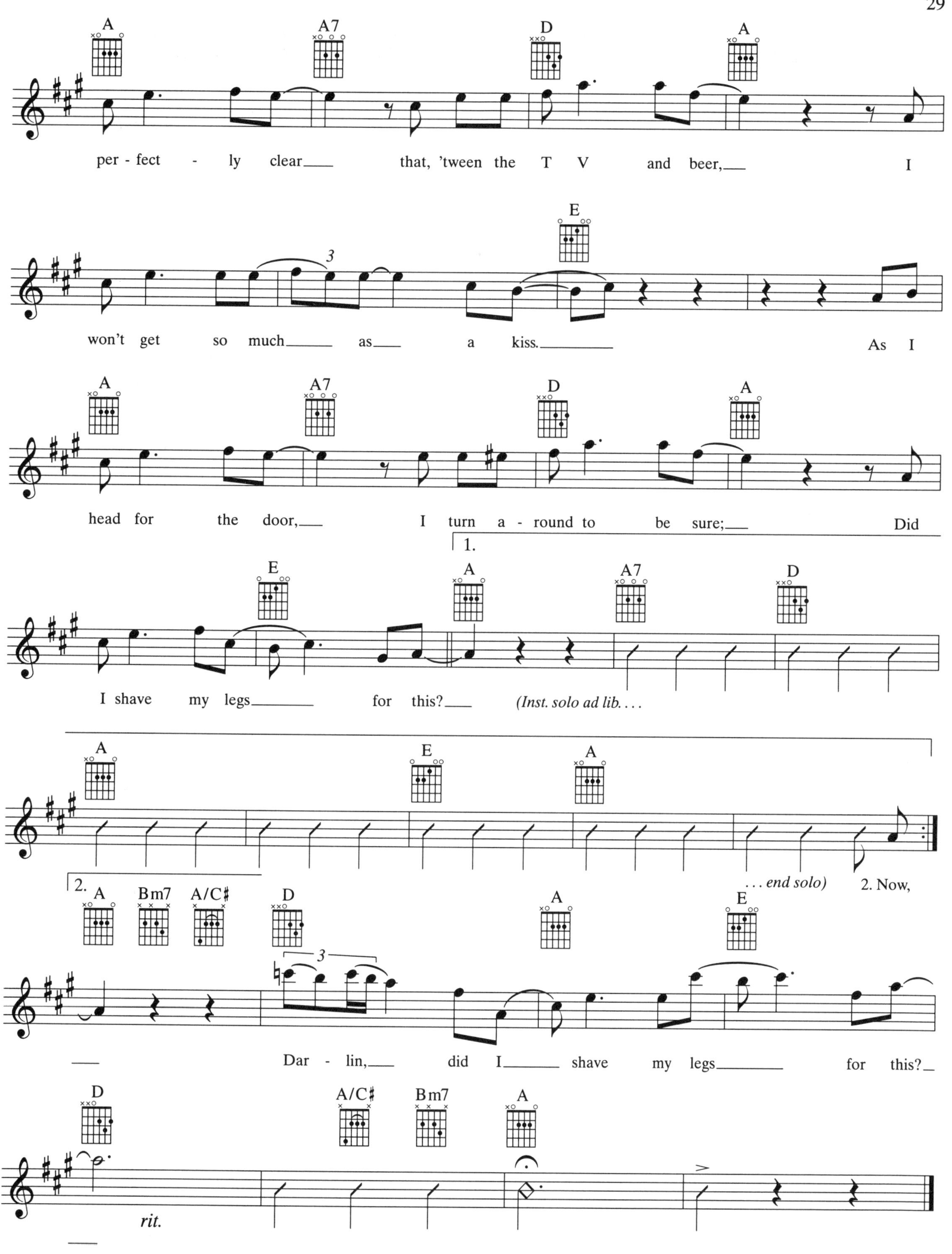

Verse 2:
Now, when we first met, you promised we'd get
A house on a hill with a pool.
Well, this trailer stays wet and we're swimming in debt.
Now you want me to go back to school.
(To Chorus:)

DON'T ROCK THE JUKEBOX

Verse 2:
I ain't got nothin' against rock and roll,
But when your heart's been broken
You need a song that's slow.
Ain't nothin' like a steel guitar
To drown a memory.
Before you spend your money, baby,
Play a song for me.
(To Chorus:)

DON'T TAKE THE GIRL

Words and Music by
CRAIG MARTIN and LARRY W. JOHNSON

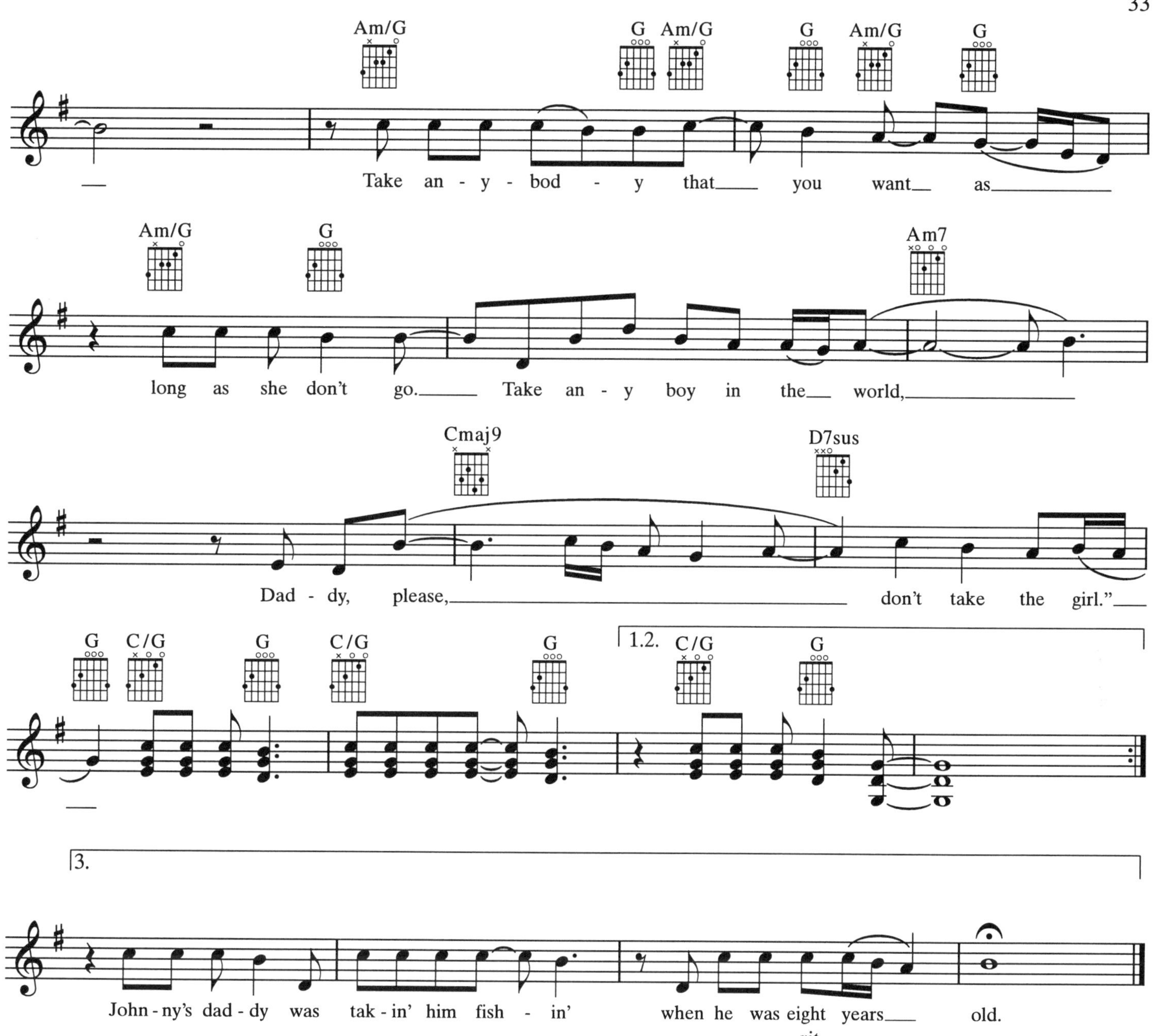

Verse 2:
Same ol' boy, same sweet girl, ten years down the road.
He held her tight and kissed her lips in front of the picture show.
A stranger came and pulled a gun and grabbed her by the arm.
Said, "If you do what I tell you to, there won't be any harm."
And Johnny said,
"Take my money, take my wallet, take my credit cards.
Here's the watch that my grandpa gave me, here's the keys to my car.
Mister, give it a whirl, but please, don't take the girl."

Verse 3:
Same ol' boy, same sweet girl, five years down the road.
There's gonna be a little one and she says, "It's time to go."
Doctor said, "The baby's fine but, you'll have to leave
'Cause his mama's fadin' fast."
And Johnny hit his knees and then he prayed,
"Take the very breath you gave me, take the heart from my chest.
I'll gladly take her place if you'll have me.
Make this my last request.
Take me out of this world, God, please, don't take the girl."

FAST AS YOU

Tune down 1/2 step:

Words and Music by
DWIGHT YOAKAM

Moderately ♩ = 128

E

Verse:

E

1. May-be some day I'll___ be strong.___
2.3. *See additional lyrics*

May - be it won't___ be___ long.___

A

I'll be the one___ who's tough.___

E

You'll be the one___ who's got it rough.___

F♯m It won't be long and A may-be I'll be___ real E strong.___

Bridge:

A

You'll con - trol me and oh, so bold - ly, rule me till I'm free.___

E

A

Till the pain that shakes me

Verse 2:
Maybe I'll do things right,
Maybe I'll start tonight.
You'll learn to cry like me.
Baby, let's just wait and see.
Maybe I'll start tonight
And do things right.
(To Bridge:)

Verse 3:
Instrumental ad lib.
(To Bridge:)

FEELS LIKE HOME

Bm7
Bm7/E
A
D
Bm7/E
but it feels like home.
A
A/C♯
D(9)
A/C♯
In your eyes, I know what I can be. You o - pened up your heart to
Bm7
Bm7/E
1.
A
me, oh, and it feels like home. When I'm
C6
Bm7
A
2.
A
with you, ba - by, it feels like home. home. Does-n't
Bridge:
D(9)
A/C♯
mat - ter where I've been or what I've been through. 'Cause I know I've been
Bm7
C6
Bm7/E
wait-ing ev-'ry day of my life to be with you, to be with you.
Chorus:
C
C/E
In your arms I know where I be - long.

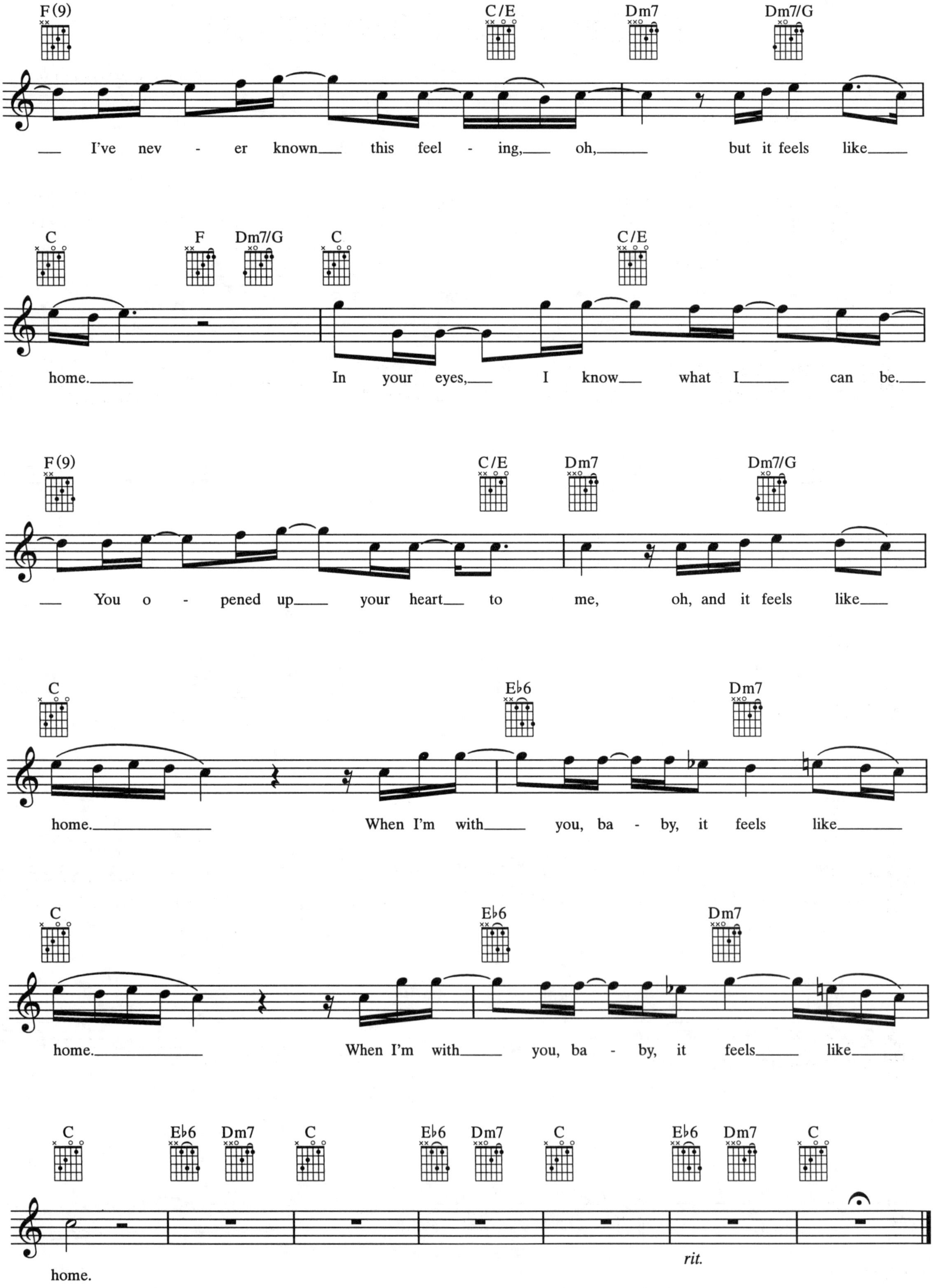

F(9) C/E Dm7 Dm7/G
I've nev - er known this feel - ing, oh, but it feels like
C F Dm7/G C C/E
home. In your eyes, I know what I can be.
F(9) C/E Dm7 Dm7/G
You o - pened up your heart to me, oh, and it feels like
C E♭6 Dm7
home. When I'm with you, ba - by, it feels like
C E♭6 Dm7
home. When I'm with you, ba - by, it feels like
C E♭6 Dm7 C E♭6 Dm7 C E♭6 Dm7 C
home.
rit.

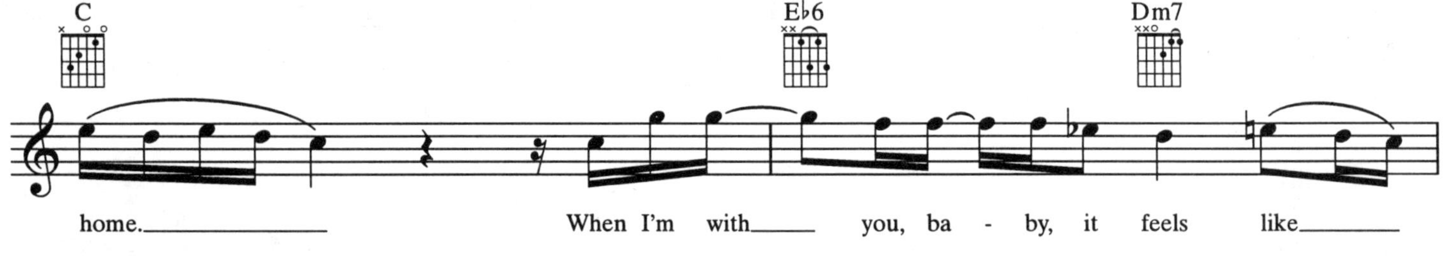

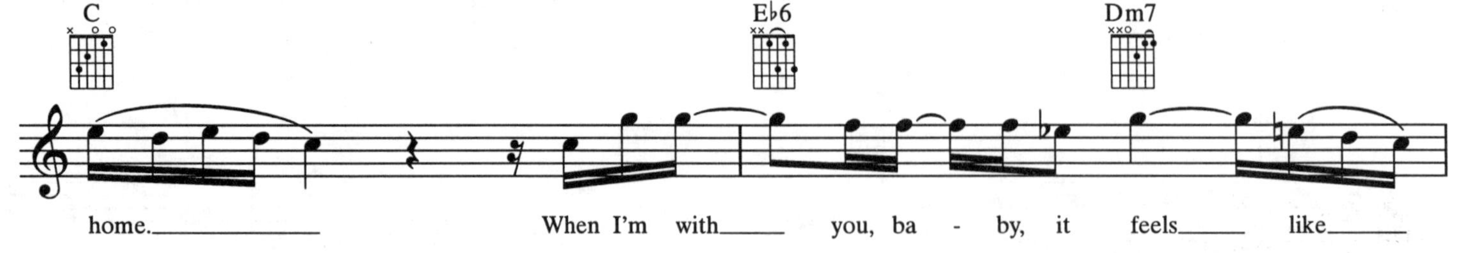

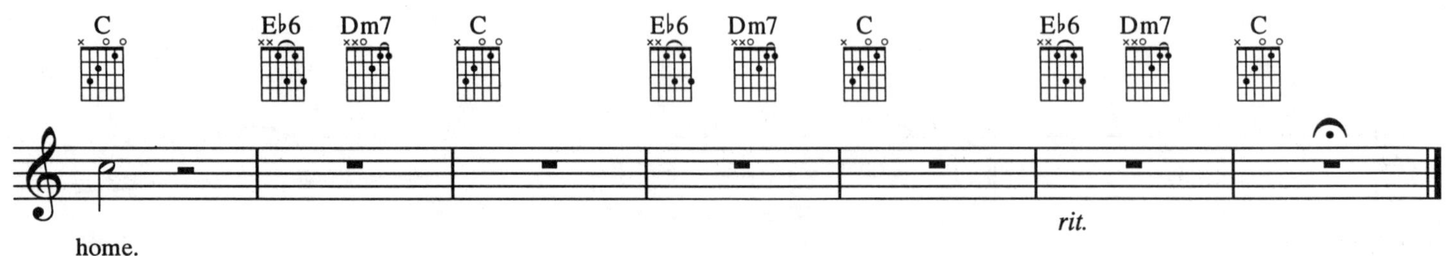

FROM THIS MOMENT ON

Words and Music by
SHANIA TWAIN and R.J. LANGE

D
G
wait to live my life with you, can't wait to start.
C (9)
You and I will nev - er be a - part. My dreams
Em7
C (9)
G
came true be - cause of you.
Verse 3:
G/D
D
N.C.
A(9)
E
From this mo - ment, as long as I live, I will
D
E
love you, I prom - ise you this. There is noth -
D
A
Bm
E
D(9)
- ing I would - n't give, from this mo - ment on.
A
F♯m7
D(9)
E
Chorus:
A
D
You're the rea - son I be - lieve in love. And

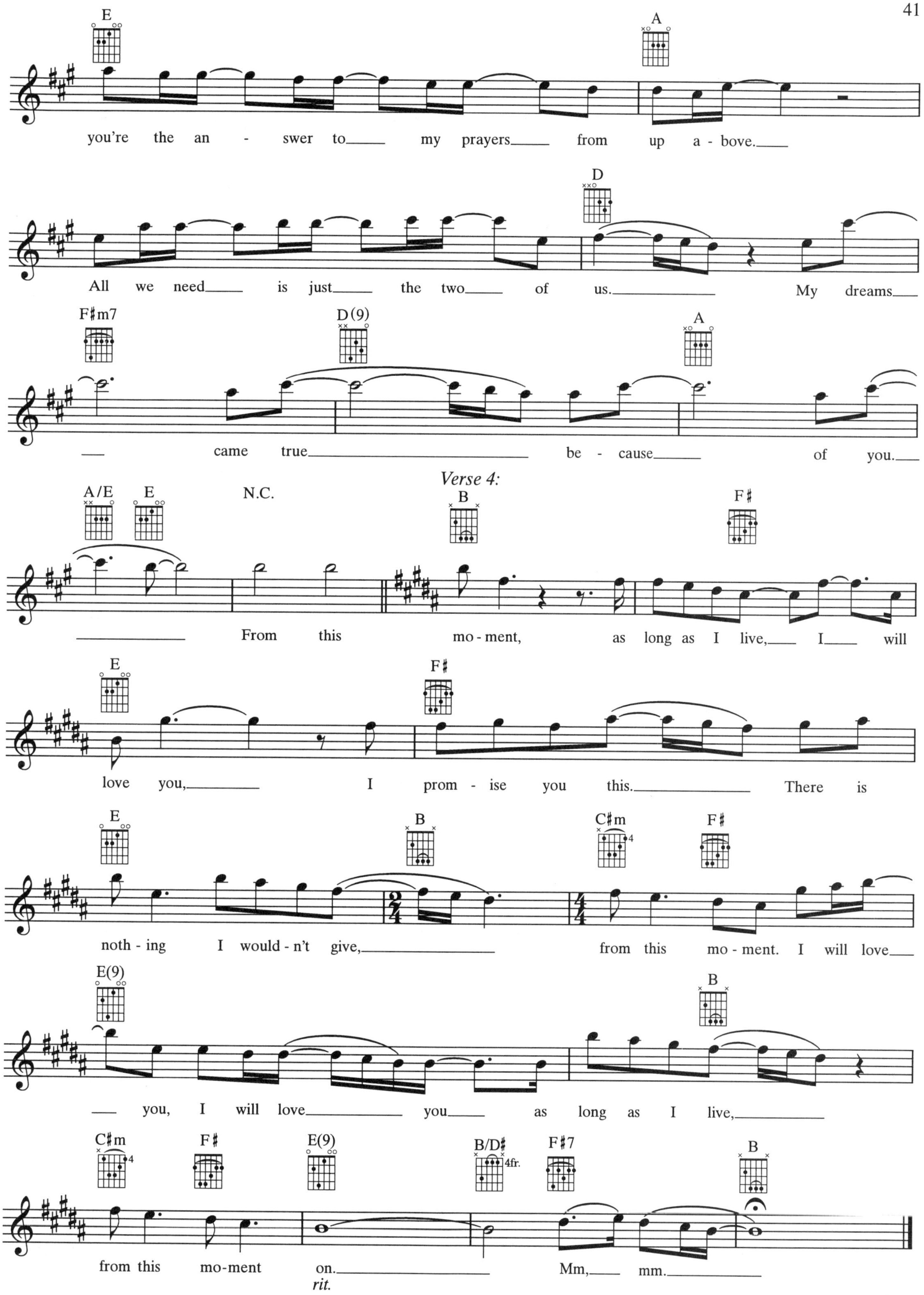

E A
you're the an - swer to___ my prayers___ from up a - bove.___

D
All we need___ is just___ the two___ of us.___ My dreams___

F♯m7 D(9) A
___ came true___ be - cause___ of you.___

Verse 4:

A/E E N.C. B F♯
___ From this mo - ment, as long as I live,___ I___ will

E F♯
love you,___ I prom - ise you this.___ There is

E B C♯m F♯
noth - ing I would - n't give,___ from this mo - ment. I will love___

E(9) B
___ you, I will love___ you___ as long as I live,___

C♯m F♯ E(9) B/D♯ F♯7 B
from this mo - ment on.___ Mm,___ mm.___
rit.

FOR YOU I WILL

Words and Music by
DIANE WARREN

Verse 2:
It's not like me at all, to talk about
The likelihood of finally settling down.
Couldn't speak the words "I love you,"
Or find the courage to say "I do."
(To Chorus:)

FOREVER'S AS FAR AS I'LL GO

Words and Music by
MIKE REID

G
F♯m
A
love it can hold.
That's all I can do.
Bm
F♯m
G(9)
G
But I've thought a - bout how long I'll love you.
D/F♯
Em
D/F♯
And it's on - ly fair that you know for -
G
G/A
ev - er's as far as I'll
1.
D
G/D
D
G/D
2.
D
go.
2. When there's
go.
F♯m
G
G/A
A
For - ev - er's as far
G/A
A
G(9)
G
as I'll go.
D/F♯
Bm
G
Repeat ad lib. and fade

GO REST HIGH ON THAT MOUNTAIN

Words and Music by
VINCE GILL

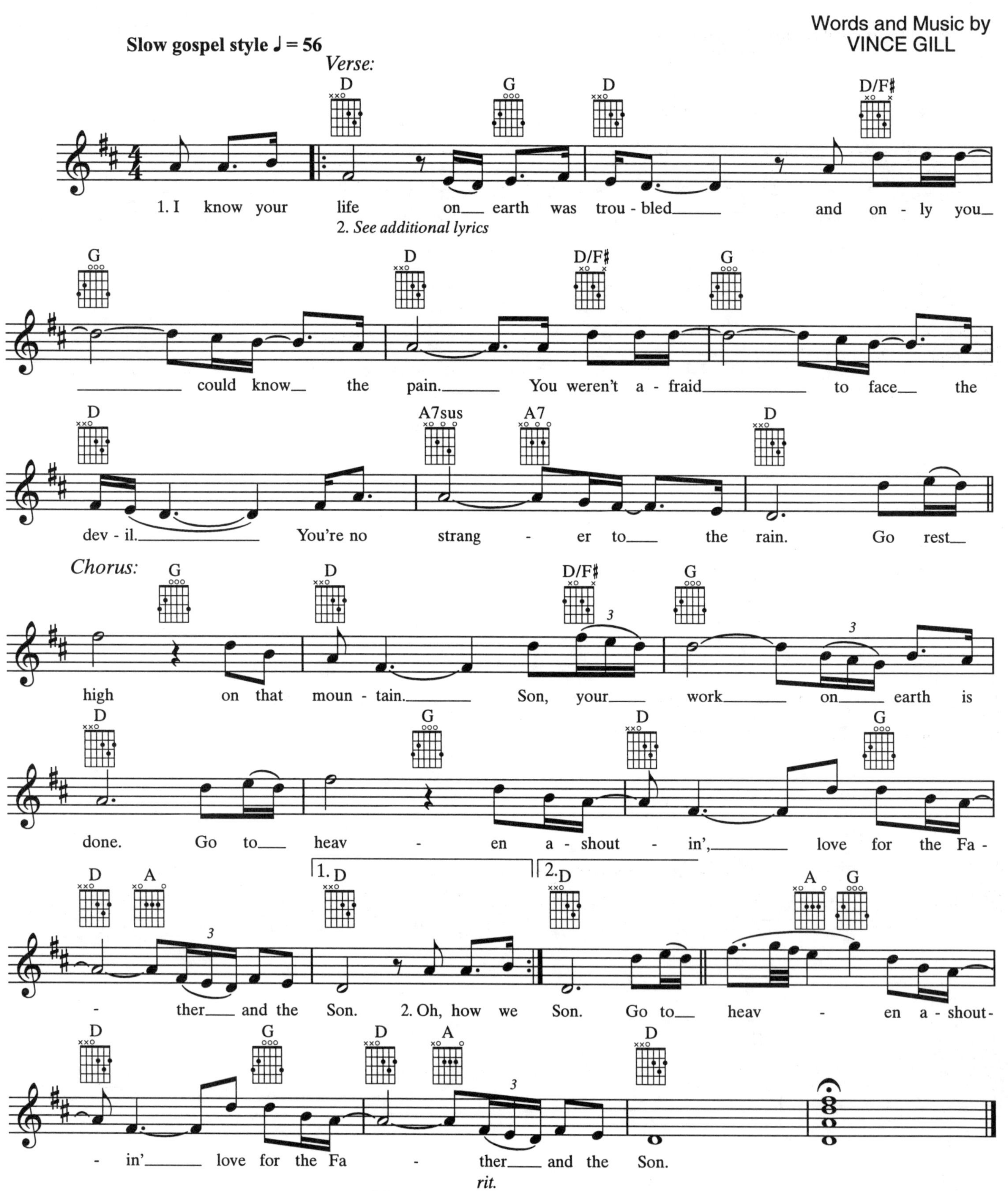

Verse 2:
Oh, how we cried the day you left us.
We gathered 'round your grave to grieve.
I wish I could see the angels' faces
When they hear your sweet voice sing.
(To Chorus:)

GFM0009

GONE COUNTRY

Chorus:

G C(9) D G

coun - try, look at them boots. She's gone coun - try,

C(9) D G C(9) D

back to her roots. She's gone coun - try, a new kind of suit. She's gone

Em *To Coda* 𝄌 1. G

coun - try, here she comes.

D C(9) G D C(9)

2. Well, the

2. G C(9) D G C(9) D

G C(9) D Em *D.S.* 𝄋 *al Coda*

3. Well, he com -

𝄌 *Coda* G D C(9) G

D C G C D

Yeah, he's gone coun - try, a new kind of walk. He's gone

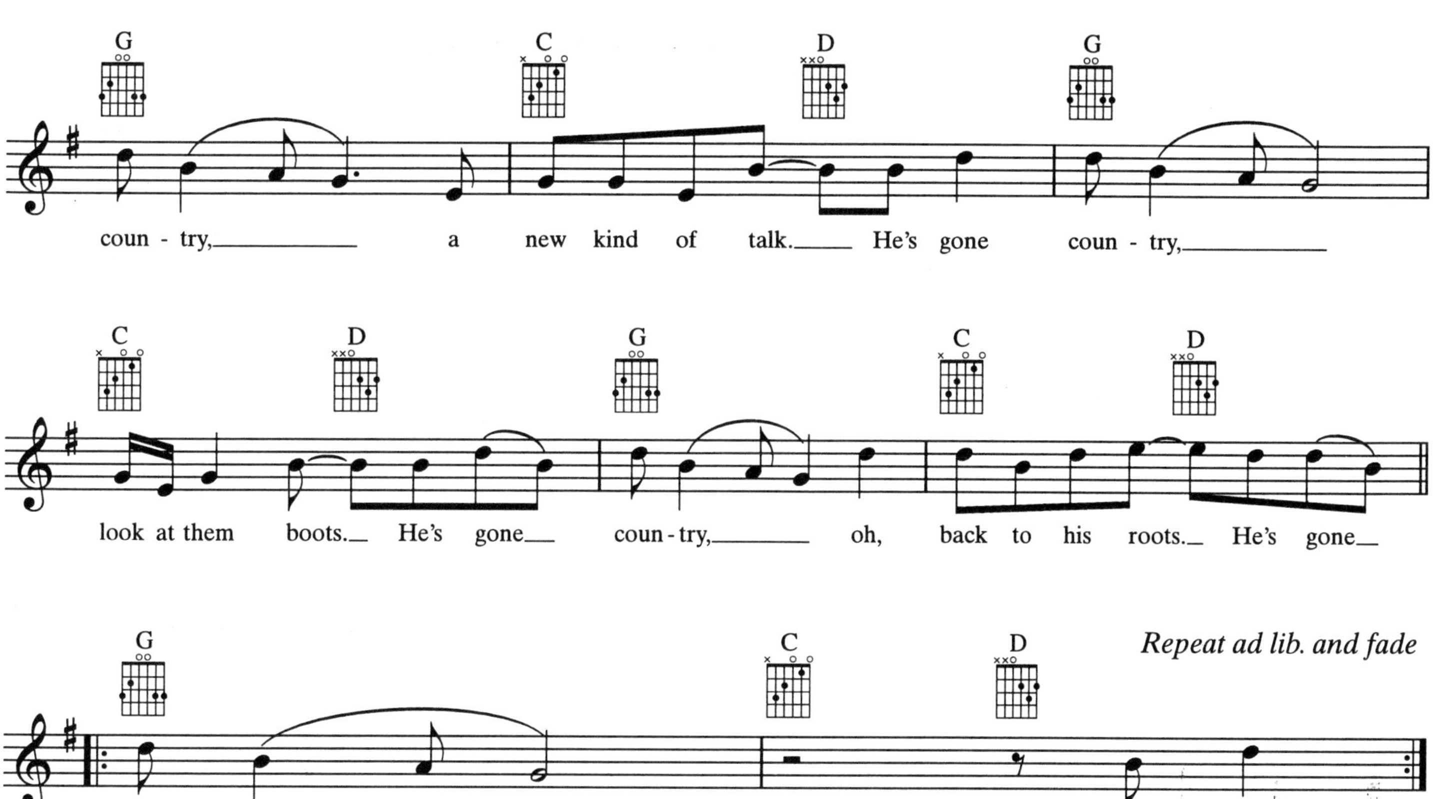

Verse 2:
Well, the folk scene's dead, but he's holding out in the village.
He's been writing songs, speaking out against wealth
and privilege.
He says, "I don't believe in money, but a man could make
him a killin'.
'Cause some of that stuff don't sound much different
than Dylan.
I hear, down there, it's changed you see.
They're not as backward as they used to be."

Chorus 2:
He's gone country, look at them boots.
He's gone country, back to his roots.
He's gone country, a new kind of suit.
He's gone country, here he comes.

Verse 3:
Well, he commutes to L.A., but he's got a house in the valley,
But the bills are piling up and the pop scene just ain't on a rally.
He says, "Honey I'm a serious composer schooled in voice and composition,
But with the crime and the smog these days this ain't
No place for children.
Lord, it sounds so easy, this shouldn't take long.
Be back in the money in no time at all."
(To Chorus 2:)

GOD BLESSED TEXAS

Written by
PORTER HOWELL and BRADY SEALS

Verse 2:
First he let the sun shine,
Then he made the waters deep.
Then he gave us moonlight
For all the world to see.
Well, everybody knows that that Lord works in mysterious ways.
He took a rest, then on the very next day . . .
(To Chorus:)

HOLES IN THE FLOOR OF HEAVEN

Verse 2:
Seasons come and seasons go,
Nothing stays the same.
I grew up, fell in love,
Met a girl who took my name.
Year by year we made a life
In this sleepy, little town.
I thought we'd grow old together.
Lord, I sure do miss her now.
(To Chorus:)

Verse 3:
Well, my little girl is twenty-three,
I walk her down the aisle.
It's a shame her mom can't be here now
To see her lovely smile.
They throw the rice, I catch her eye
As the rain starts coming down.
She takes my hand, says, "Daddy, don't be sad,
'Cause I know Mama's watching now."
(To Chorus:)

HONEY, I'M HOME

Words and Music by
SHANIA TWAIN and R.J. LANGE

Moderate country rock ♩= 72

Verses 2 & 3:

E

when I thought things could - n't get worse, I re - al - ized I for -

3. *See additional lyrics*

worth the pay.
Can't wait till the end of the day.
B
Hey, hon - ey, I'm on my way.
Hey! (Hey!) Hey! (Hey!) Hey! Hey! Hey!
Chorus:
E
Hon - ey, I'm home and I had a hard day. Pour me a cold one and,
oh, by the way:
B
rub my feet, gim - me some - thing to eat.
Fix me up my fa - v'rite treat.
E
Hon - ey, I'm back, my head's
kill - ing me. I need to re - lax and watch T V. Get
B
off the phone, give the dog a bone. Hey! (Hey!)

Verse 3:
I broke a nail opening the mail.
I cursed out loud 'cause it hurt like hell.
This job's a pain, it's so mundane.
It sure don't stimulate my brain.
This job ain't worth the pay.
Can't wait till the end of the day.
Hey, honey, I'm on my way.
Hey! (Hey!) Hey! (Hey!)
Hey! Hey! Hey!
(To Chorus:)

I CAN STILL FEEL YOU

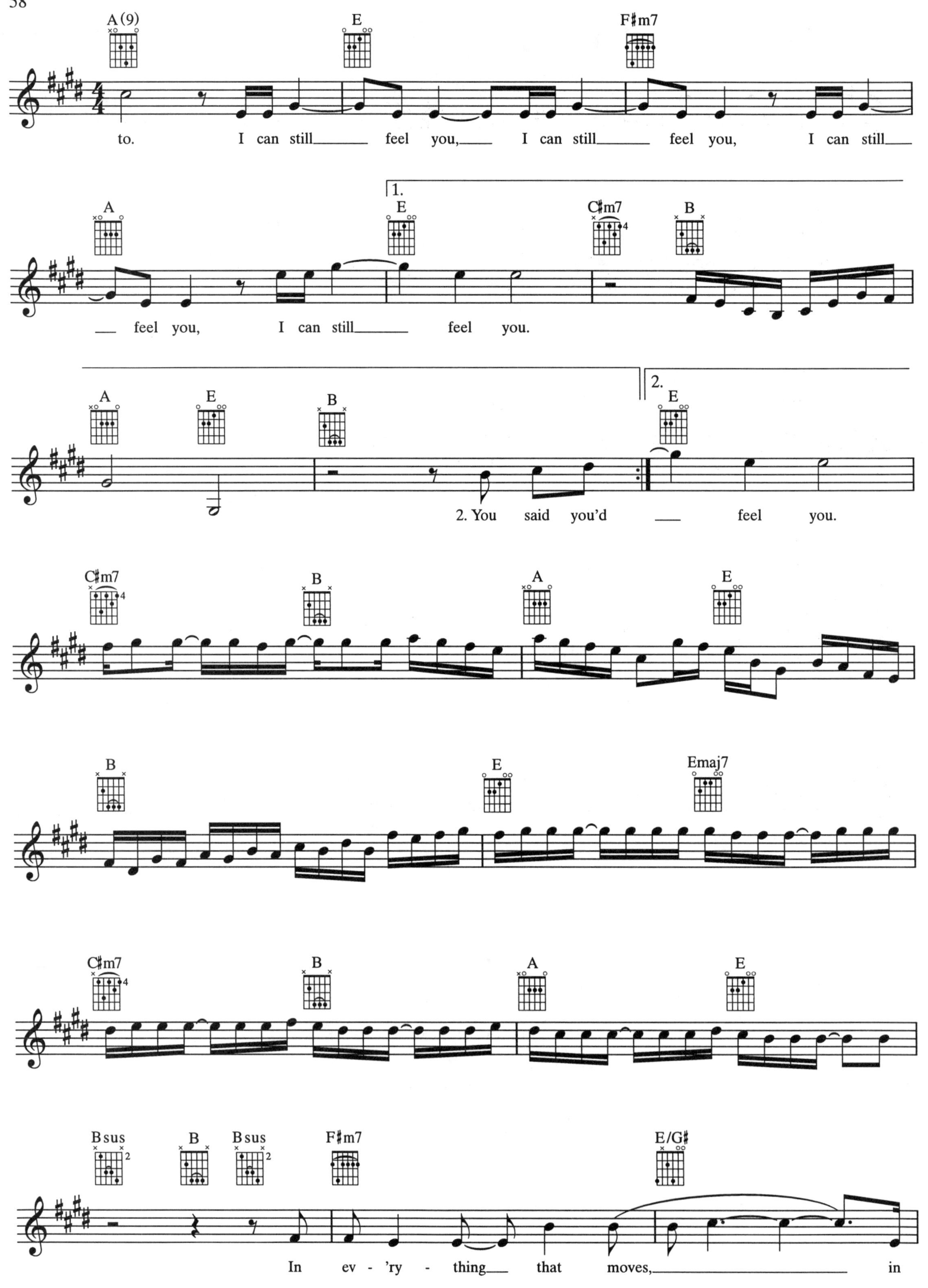
A(9)
E
F♯m7
to. I can still feel you, I can still feel you, I can still
A
1.
E
C♯m7
B
feel you, I can still feel you.
A
E
B
2.
E
2. You said you'd feel you.
C♯m7
B
A
E
B
E
Emaj7
C♯m7
B
A
E
Bsus
B
Bsus
F♯m7
E/G♯
In ev - 'ry - thing that moves, in

Verse 2:
You said you'd love me forever,
Then you said it's over
And left me without the missing link.
I thought I'd forget you
But I guess I forgot to.
And lately I've been too confused to think.
When I reach for someone new,
It's like I'm touching you.
(To Chorus:)

HOW DO I LIVE

Words and Music by
DIANE WARREN

Verse 2:
Without you, there'd be no sun in my sky,
There would be no love in my life,
There'd be no world left for me.
And I, baby, I don't know what I would do,
I'd be lost if I lost you.
If you ever leave,
Baby, you would take away everything real in my life.
And tell me now . . .
(To Chorus:)

I CAN LOVE YOU LIKE THAT

Words and Music by
STEVE DIAMOND, MARIBETH DERRY
and JENNIFER KIMBALL

A C♯m D
be all that you need, show you you're ev - 'ry - thing that's pre - cious to me.
G E7sus 1. A
If you give me a chance, I can love you like that.
D E7sus 2. A
2. I
Bridge:
Em7
You want ten - der - ness, I've got ten -
Bm7 A
- der - ness and I see through to the heart of you. If you
Em7 Bm7 D E7sus
want a man who un - der - stands, you don't have to look ver - y far.
E
I can love you. I, I can love you like that.
Chorus:
A
I would make you my world,
C♯m D E7sus
move heav - en and earth if you were my girl. I will give you my heart,
Repeat ad lib. and fade
A C♯m D E7sus
be all that you need, show you you're ev - 'ry-thing that's pre-cious to me. I can love you like that.

I DON'T EVEN KNOW YOUR NAME

Words and Music by
ALAN JACKSON, RON JACKSON
and ANDY LOFTIN

E
F♯m7
Gdim7
E7/G♯
nev - er been_ too good at all_ those sex - u - al games. So
A
may - be it's_ just bet - ter if_ we leave it this way._ I'm in
E
N.C.
B
love with you, ba - by and I don't e - ven know_ your name.
A7
E7
Instrumental
To Coda
1.
B7
2. So I
Slow shuffle ♩ = 100
Bridge:
2.
The next thing I re - mem - ber, I was
hear - in' wed - ding bells, stand - in' by a wom - an in a long,_ white, lac - y veil. I

Verse 2:
So I ordered straight tequilla, a little courage in the shot.
I asked you for a date and then I asked to tie the knot.
I got a little wasted, yeah, I went a little far.
But I finally got to hug you when you helped me to my car.
The last thing I remember I heard myself say:
I'm in love with you, baby, and I don't even know your name.
(To Chorus 2:)

Chorus 3:
Yeah, I'm married to a waitress; I don't even know her name.
I've never been too good at all those sexual games.
I never thought my love life would quite turn out this way.
Hey, I'm married to a waitress and I don't even know her name.

I DON'T WANT TO MISS A THING

To Coda
Am7
C
D
the sweet-est dreams would nev - er do.
I'd still miss you, ba - by, and I don't want a miss a thing.
G
D/F♯
Em7
Lay - ing
Verse 2:
G
D/F♯
Em7
close to you, feel - ing your heart beat - ing, and I'm
C
G/B
Am7
won - d'ring what you're dream - ing, won - d'ring if it's me you're see - ing. Then I
G
D/F♯
Em7
kiss your eyes and thank God we're to - geth - er. I just wan - na
Bm7
C maj7
Dsus
D.S. al Coda
stay with you in this mo - ment for - ev - er, for - ev - er and ev - er.
Bridge:
Coda
G
F
I don't wan - na miss one smile; I don't wan - na
C/E
E♭
miss one kiss. I just wan - na be with you, right here with you,

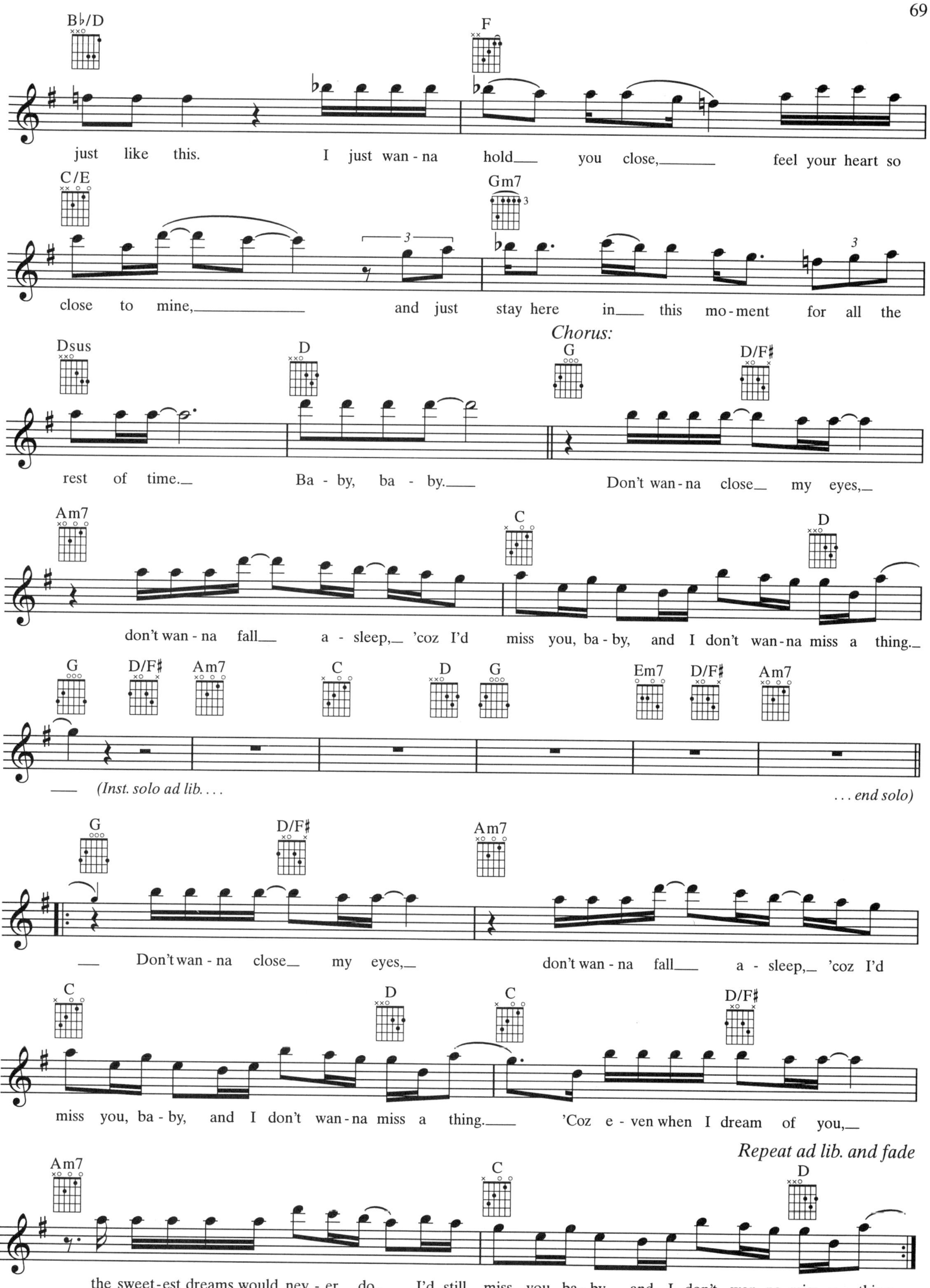
B♭/D
F
just like this. I just wan-na hold you close, feel your heart so
C/E
Gm7
close to mine, and just stay here in this mo-ment for all the
Chorus:
Dsus
D
G
D/F♯
rest of time. Ba-by, ba-by. Don't wan-na close my eyes,
Am7
C
D
don't wan-na fall a-sleep, 'coz I'd miss you, ba-by, and I don't wan-na miss a thing.
G
D/F♯
Am7
C
D
G
Em7
D/F♯
Am7
(Inst. solo ad lib....
...end solo)
G
D/F♯
Am7
Don't wan-na close my eyes, don't wan-na fall a-sleep, 'coz I'd
C
D
C
D/F♯
miss you, ba-by, and I don't wan-na miss a thing. 'Coz e-ven when I dream of you,
Repeat ad lib. and fade
Am7
C
D
the sweet-est dreams would nev-er do. I'd still miss you, ba-by, and I don't wan-na miss a thing.

I STILL BELIEVE IN YOU

Words and Music by
VINCE GILL and JOHN BARLOW JARVIS

I Still Believe in You - 2 - 1
GFM0009

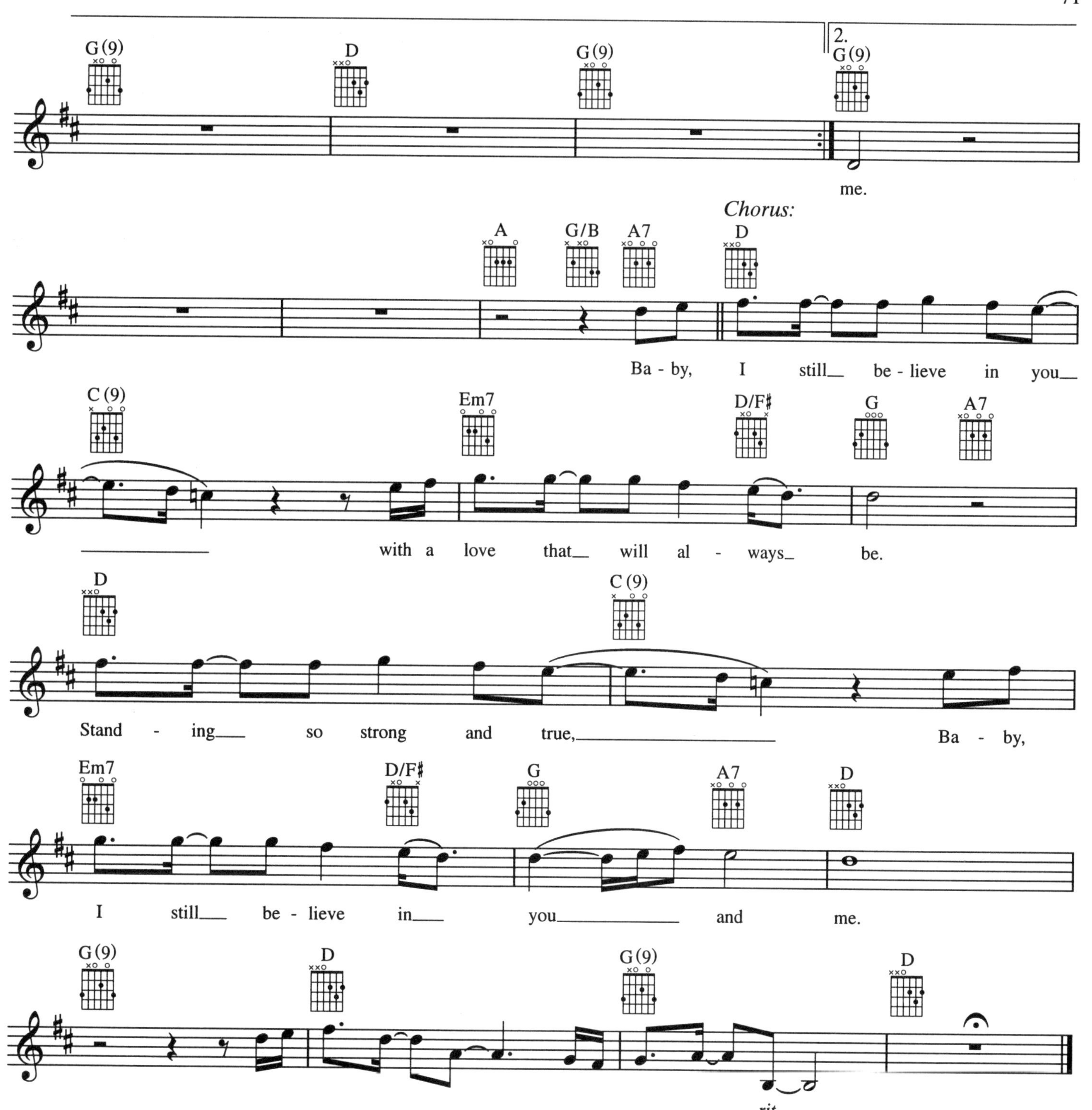

Verse 2:
Somewhere along the way, I guess I just lost track,
Only thinkin' of myself, never lookin' back.
For all the times I've hurt you, I apologize,
I'm sorry it took so long to finally realize.
Give me the chance to prove
That nothing's worth losing you.
(To Chorus:)

I SWEAR

Words and Music by
GARY BAKER and FRANK MYERS

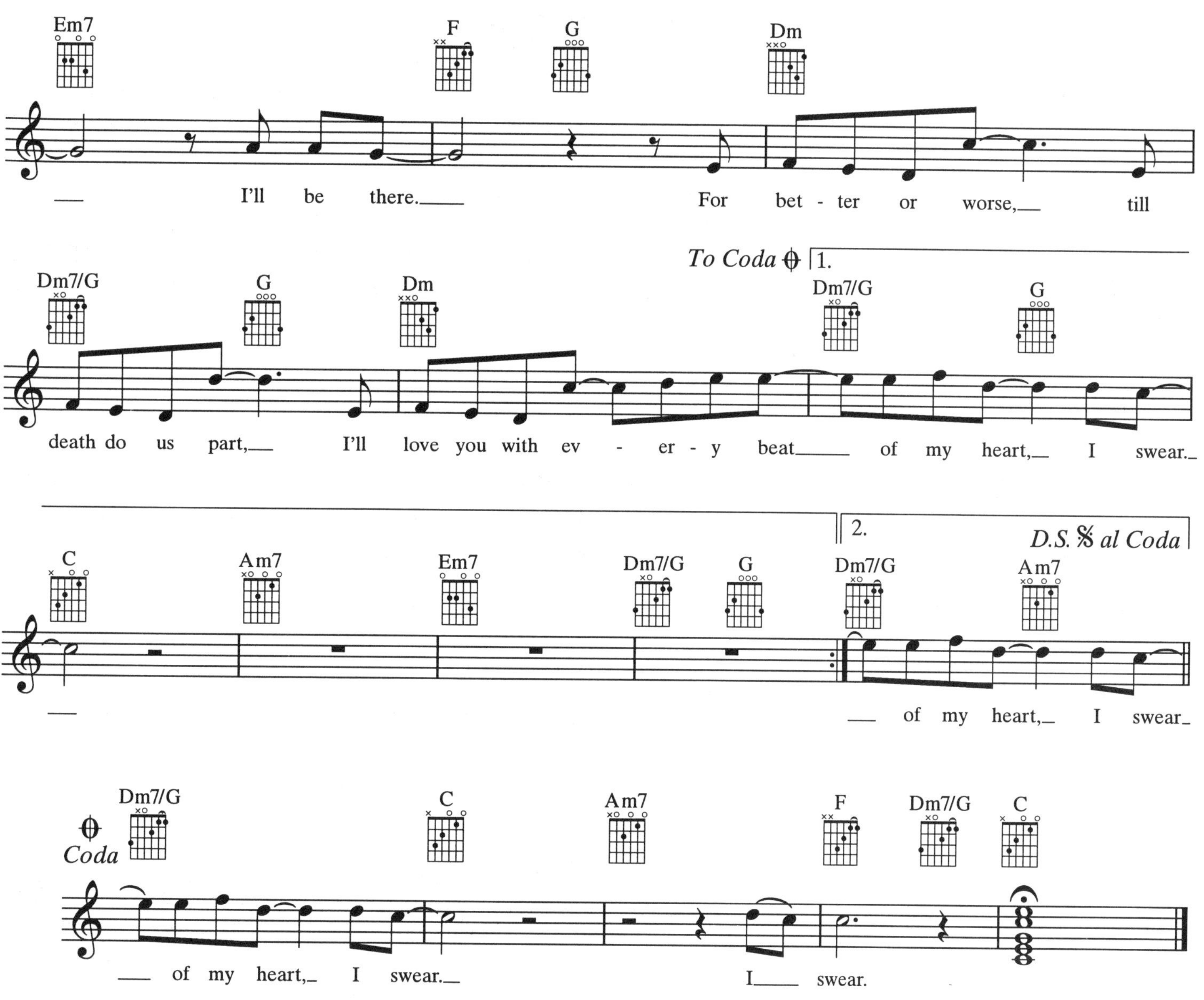

Verse 2:
I'll give you everything I can,
I'll build your dreams with these two hands
And we'll hang some memories on the wall.
And when there's silver in your hair,
You won't have to ask if I still care,
'Cause as time turns the page my love won't age at all.
(To Chorus:)

I WILL ALWAYS LOVE YOU

Words and Music by
DOLLY PARTON

Chorus:
Ab
Fm
Db
Eb
Ab
Fm
I will al - ways love you. I will al -
Db
Eb
Ab
Db/Ab
Ab
- ways love you. I hope
Verse 3:
Ab
Eb/G
Fm
Ab/Eb
life treats you kind and I hope you have all you dream
Db
Eb
Ab
Eb/G
of. I wish you joy and hap-pi - ness, but a -
Fm
Ab/Eb
Db
Eb
Bm7/E
E7
bove all this I wish you love. Oh, and
Chorus:
A
F♯m
D
E
A
F♯m
I will al - ways love you. I will
D
E
A
F♯m
D
E
al - ways love you. I will al - ways love
A
F♯m
D
E
A
you. I will al - ways love you.

I'LL TRY

Words and Music by
ALAN JACKSON

Verse 2:
So, I'm not scared; it's worth a chance to me.
Take my hand; let's face eternity.
Well, I can't tell you that I'll never change.
But I can swear that in every way. . .
(To Chorus:)

Verse 3 (second half):
I'm not perfect; just another man.
But I will give you all that I am.
(To Chorus:)

IF YOU EVER HAVE FOREVER IN MIND

Words and Music by
VINCE GILL and TROY SEALS

Verse 2:
Music has ended, still you wanna dance.
I know that feeling, I can't take the chance.
You live for the moment; no future, no past.
I may be a fool to live by the rules.
I want it to last.
(To Chorus:)

IN ANOTHER'S EYES

Words and Music by
BOBBY WOOD, JOHN PEPPARD
and GARTH BROOKS

Verse 2:
In another's eyes, I can do no wrong.
He believes in me and his faith is strong.
I'd never fall or even compromise,
In another's eyes.
(To Chorus:)

IN THIS LIFE

Words and Music by
MIKE REID and ALLEN SHAMBLIN

In This Life - 2 - 1
GFM0009

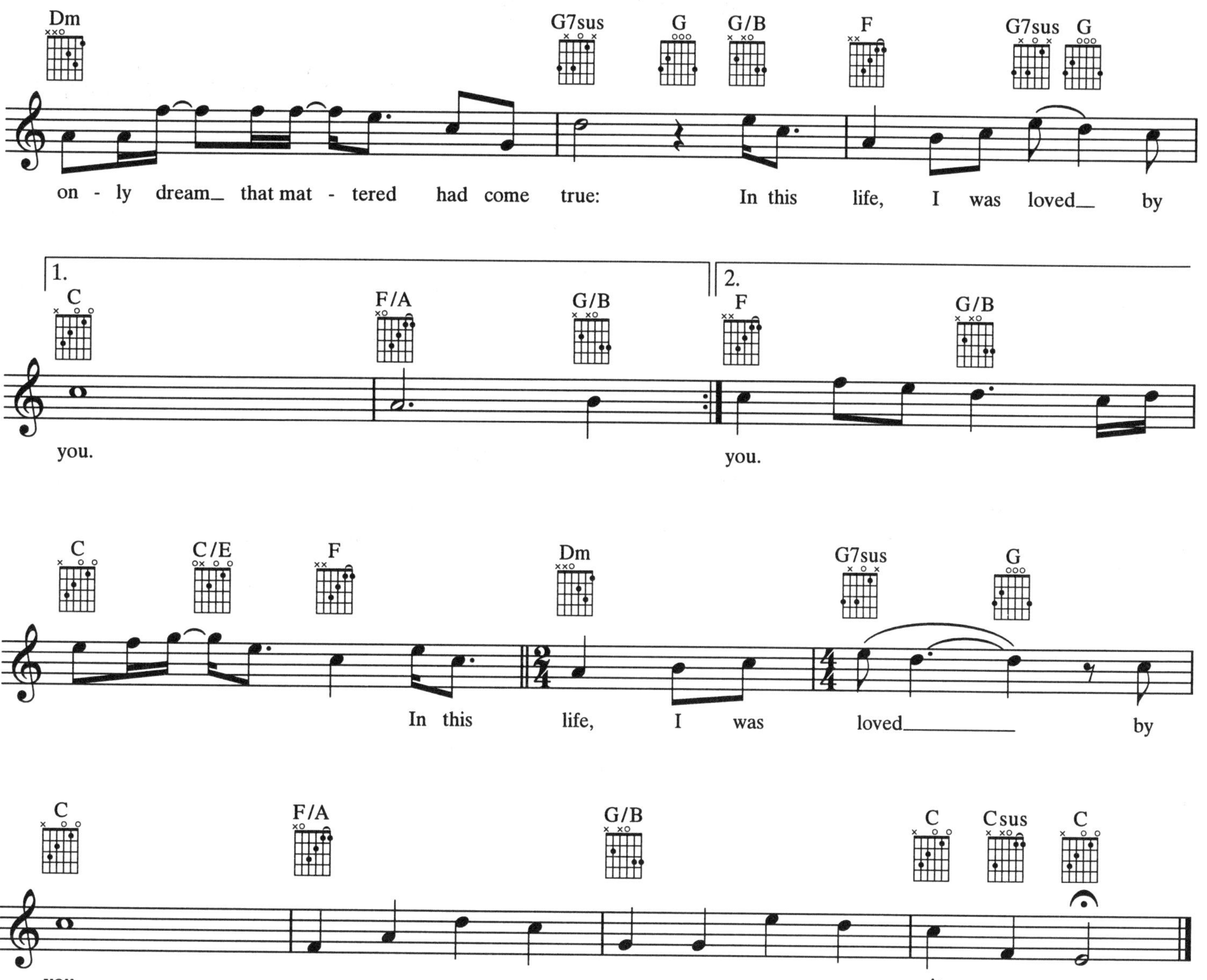
Dm
G7sus
G
G/B
F
G7sus
G
on - ly dream_ that mat - tered had come true:
In this life, I was loved_ by
1.
C
F/A
G/B
2.
F
G/B
you.
you.
C
C/E
F
Dm
G7sus
G
In this life, I was loved_________ by
C
F/A
G/B
C
Csus
C
you.
rit.

INDIAN OUTLAW

Words and Music by
GENE SIMMONS, TOMMY BARNES
and JOHN D. LOUDERMILK

E B A E5
B5 A5 E5
3. I ain't look-in' for trou-
Verses 3 & 4:
B5
- ble, we can ride my po - ny dou - ble, make your lit - tle heart
4. See additional lyrics
A5 Em D Em
bub-ble, girl, like a glass of wine. Well, I re-mem-ber the med-
E5 B5
- i - cine man, he caught Run-ning Wa - ter in my hands, drug me a - round by my
A5 Em D Em
head - band, said I was - n't her kind. 'Cause I'm an In - di - an out -
E5 B5
- law, half Cher - o - kee and Choc - taw. My ba - by, she's a
1.
A5 E5
Chip-pe - wa, she's a one-of - a - kind. 4. Well, I can kill a deer or

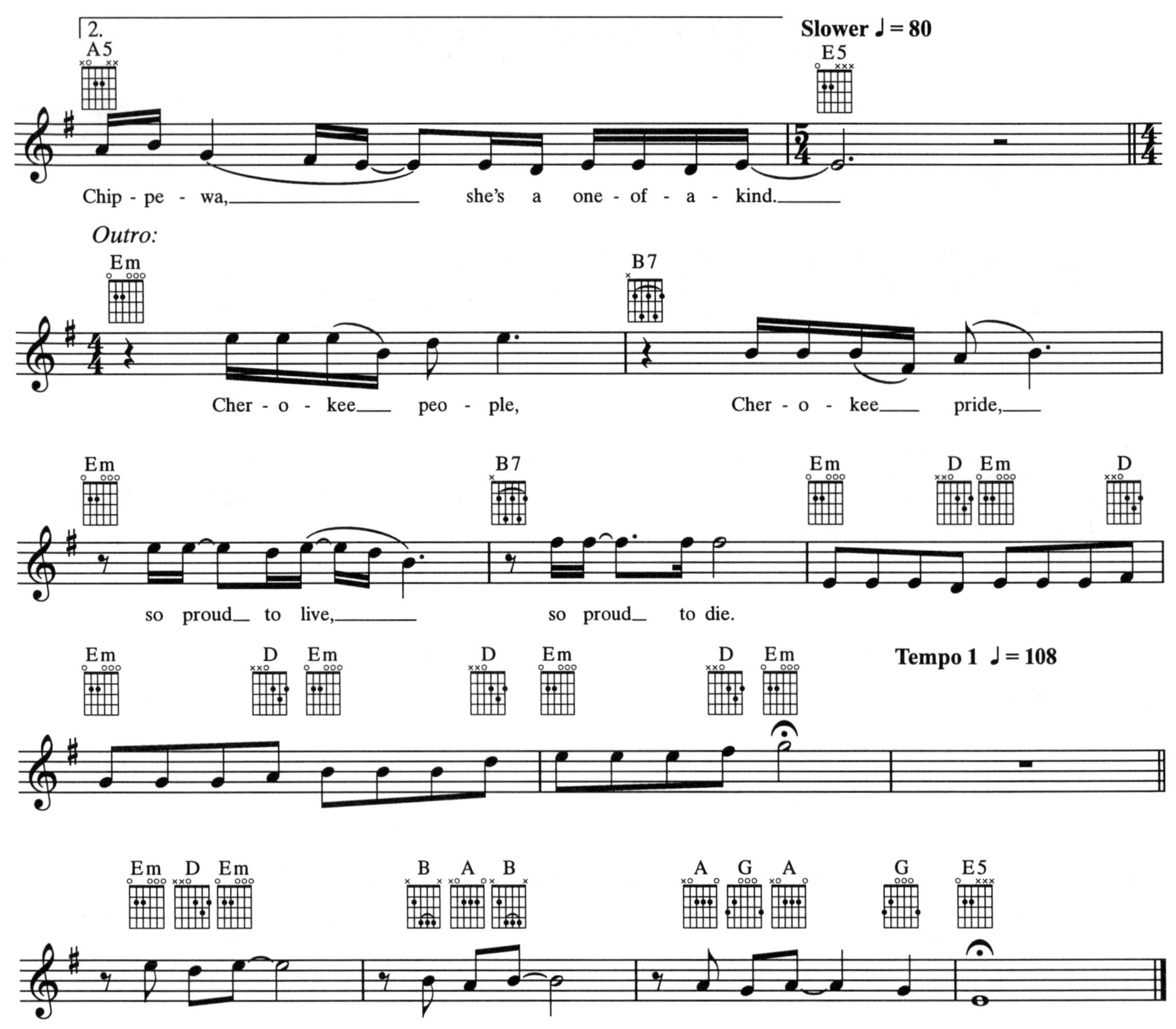

Verse 2:
You can find me in my wigwam, I'll be beating on my tom-tom.
Pull out the pipe and smoke you some, hey, and pass it around.
'Cause I'm an Indian outlaw, half Cherokee and Choctaw.
My baby, she's a Chippewa, she's a one-of-a-kind.
(To Verse 3:)

Verse 4:
Well, I can kill a deer or buffalo with just my arrow and my hickory bow
From a hundred yards, don't you know, I do it all of the time.
They all gather 'round my teepee late at night tryin' to catch a peek at me
In nothin' but my buffalo briefs, I got 'em standin' in line.
'Cause I'm an Indian outlaw, half Cherokee and Choctaw.
My baby, she's a Chippewa, she's a one-of-a-kind.
(To Outro:)

DON'T FENCE ME IN

Words and Music by
COLE PORTER

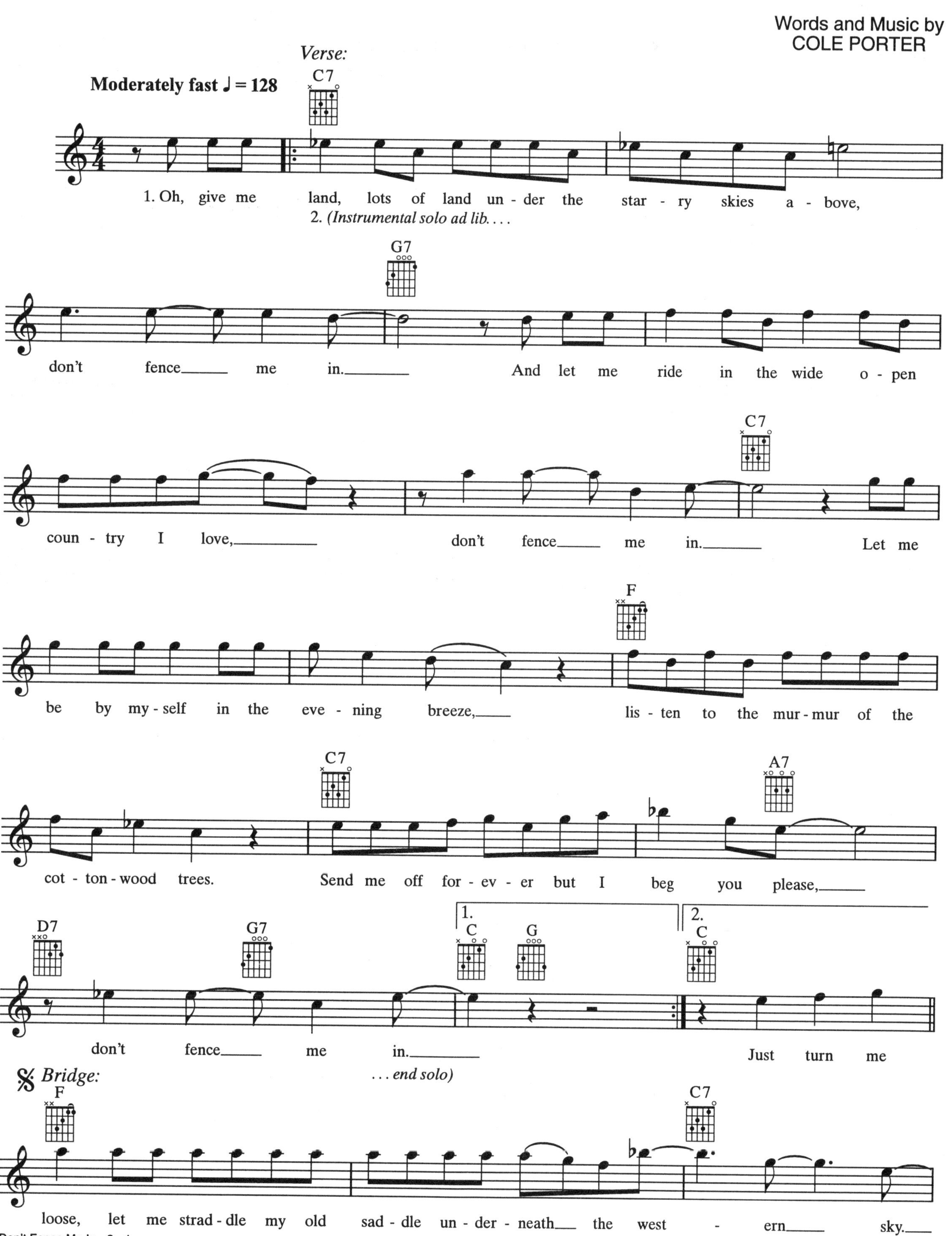

F
Let me won - der o - ver yon - der 'til I see___ the moun -
G7
C7
- tains___ rise.___ I want to ride to the ridge where the
F
west com - menc - es, gaze at the moon 'til I lose___ my sens - es.
C7
A7
D7
G7
To Coda
C
N.C.
Look at hob-bles and I can't stand fenc - es. Don't fence me___ in.
D7
A7
D
G7
D7
B7
E7
A7
D7
E7

A7
E7
A7
D7
A7
F♯7
B7
E7
A7
D.S. 𝄋 al Coda
Just turn me
𝄌 Coda
C7
in.
G7
Don't fence me in.
C7
Don't fence me in.
F
F♯7
C7
A7
D7
G7
D7
G7
D7
G7
C
Don't fence me, don't fence me, don't fence me in.
F
G7
C7
C9

JUST TO HEAR YOU SAY THAT YOU LOVE ME

Verse 2:
If I could taste your kiss,
There'd be no sweeter gift heaven could offer, baby.
I want to be the one
Living to give you love.
I'd walk across this world just to be
Close to you, 'cause I want you close to me.
(To Chorus:)

KICK A LITTLE

Words and Music by
PORTER HOWELL, DWAYNE O'BRIEN
and BRADY SEALS

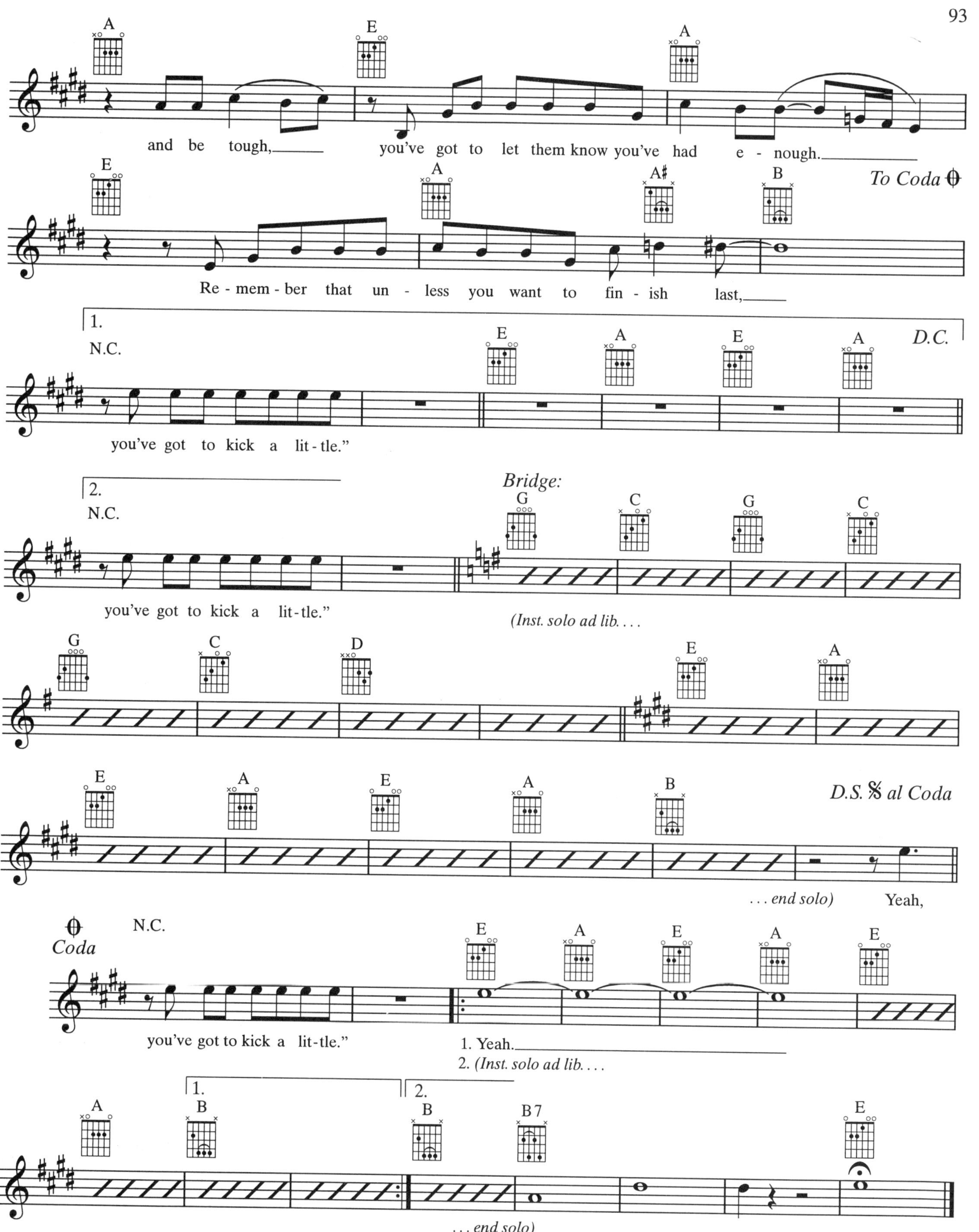

Verse 2:
Some people judge you by the way you look;
They see you once and say you ain't no good.
Feels like they're never gonna take you for who you are.
That's when you have to stand up and be strong
And go the extra mile to prove them all wrong.
Just remember when they push you way too far,
(To Chorus:)

LET ME LET GO

Tune down 1/2 step:

Words and Music by
DENNIS MORGAN and STEVE DIAMOND

Let Me Let Go - 3 - 1
GFM0009

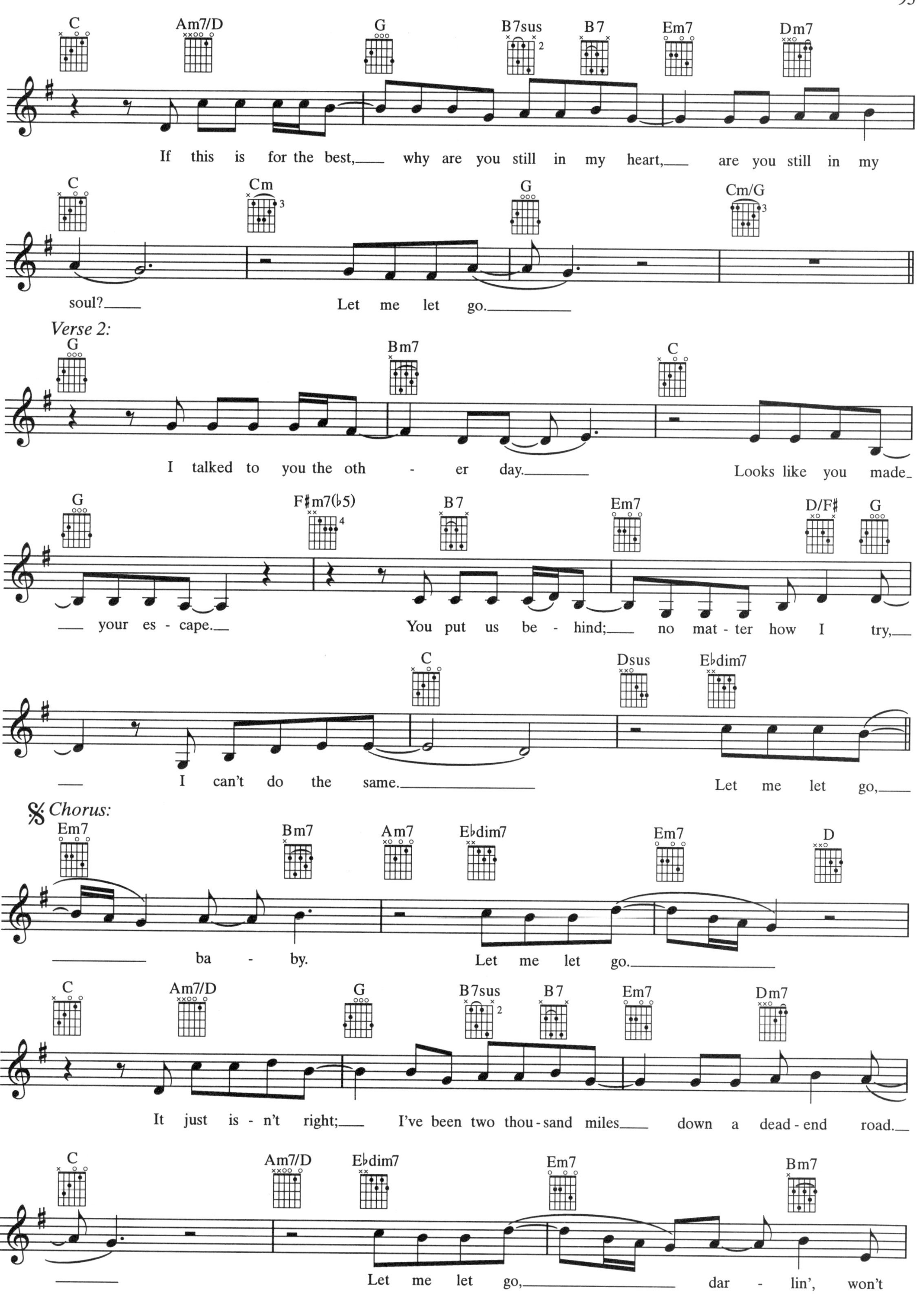
C
Am7/D
G
B7sus
B7
Em7
Dm7
If this is for the best, why are you still in my heart, are you still in my
C
Cm
G
Cm/G
soul? Let me let go.
Verse 2:
G
Bm7
C
I talked to you the oth - er day. Looks like you made
G
F♯m7(♭5)
B7
Em7
D/F♯
G
your es - cape. You put us be - hind; no mat - ter how I try,
C
Dsus
E♭dim7
I can't do the same. Let me let go,
Chorus:
Em7
Bm7
Am7
E♭dim7
Em7
D
ba - by. Let me let go.
C
Am7/D
G
B7sus
B7
Em7
Dm7
It just is - n't right; I've been two thou - sand miles down a dead - end road.
C
Am7/D
E♭dim7
Em7
Bm7
Let me let go, dar - lin', won't

Am7 E♭dim7 Em7 D C Am7/D
you? I just got - ta know, yeah. If this is for the best,
G B7sus B7 Em7 Dm7
why are you still in my heart, are you still in my
C Cm To Coda G
soul? Let me let go.
Bridge:
Dm7 Dm7/G G C(9)
The lights of this strange cit - y are shin - in', but they don't hold
Cm Bm7 Bm7/E Em7
no fas - ci - na - tion for me. I try to find the bright side, ba - by, but
Am7 G/B C Am7/D
ev - 'ry - where I look, ev - 'ry - where I turn, you're all I see.
E♭dim7 D.S. al Coda
Let me, let me let go.
Coda G
Cm/G G Cm/G G(9)
Let me let go. Let me let go.
rit.

LIFE GOES ON

Words and Music by
DEL GRAY, KEITH FOLLESE and THOM McHUGH

G/B C G D7 G
sun goes down. This old world keeps spin - nin' a - round.
G/B C G
Not much has changed since you've been gone. I miss you, hon - ey, but life
D7 G
goes on.
1.
C G
D G G/B C
2. You
2.
C
F C G
C F/C C D7
Bridge:
Em F C
Thanks to you say - in' we're through, I've got - ten
G Em F
good at get - tin' by. I don't know when, but I'll

Verse 2:
You say you can tell that I'm doin' well
By the sound of my voice.
What'd you expect, baby, when you left?
You gave me no choice.
(To Chorus:)

LONGNECK BOTTLE

Words and Music by
STEVE WARINER and RICK CARNES

Longneck Bottle - 2 - 1
GFM0009

Chorus:
D
G
D
Long - neck bot - tle, let go of my hand.
G
D
Whoa, juke - box, don't start playing that song a - gain,
G
'cause there's a girl at home who loves me, you know
D
G
D
A
she won't un - der - stand. Long - neck bot - tle, let go of my
1.
D
hand.
2.
D
hand.
There's a girl
G
G♯dim7
D/A
at home who loves me, you know she won't un - der - stand.
G
D
A
Long - neck bot - tle, let go of my
D
G
G6
F♯6
F6
E6
E♭6
D6
hand.

LOOKING THROUGH YOUR EYES

Words and Music by
CAROLE BAYER SAGER and DAVID FOSTER

Capo at 1st fret

Chorus:
D A D
Here in the night, I see the sun. Here in the dark, our two
A D A C♯7
hearts are one. It's out of our hands, we can't stop what we have be -
F♯m7 Bm7 1. Esus
gun. And love just took me by sur - prise,
E A(9) D/A E/A A(9) D/A E/A
look - ing through your eyes.
3. I
2. Esus A
look - ing through your eyes.
And there are
Bridge:
E/D D A(9) E/D D
some things we don't know, some - times a heart just needs to go.
A(9) Dmaj7 D6 C♯m7 F♯m7
And there is so much that I re - mem - ber, un - der -

Chorus:
G
E
D
neath the o - pen sky with you for - ev - er. Here in the night,
A
D
A
I see the sun. Here in the dark, our two hearts are one. It's
D
A
C♯7
F♯m7
out of our hands, we can't stop what we have be - gun. And love just took
Bm7
Esus
N.C.
me by sur - prise. look - ing through your eyes.
A(9)
D/A
E/A
A(9)
D/A
E/A
A
Look - ing through your eyes.

LOOSEN UP MY STRINGS

Words and Music by
CLINT BLACK and HAYDEN NICHOLAS

E7
B7
C7/G
B7/F♯
E7
... end solo)
Now, when it
Bridge:
E7(♯9)
comes to get - tin' down and I'm al - ways keep - in' track,
D.S. 𝄋 al Coda
I don't need some yo - yo tak - in' up my slack. The
Coda
C7/G
B7/F♯
E7
loos - en up my strings. Yeah, he'll have a
A7
E7
line on me till my fat la - dy sings.
B7
C7/G
B7/F♯
But I'll be swing - in' while I loos - en up my
E7
B7
strings. Yeah, we'll all be swing - in' while I

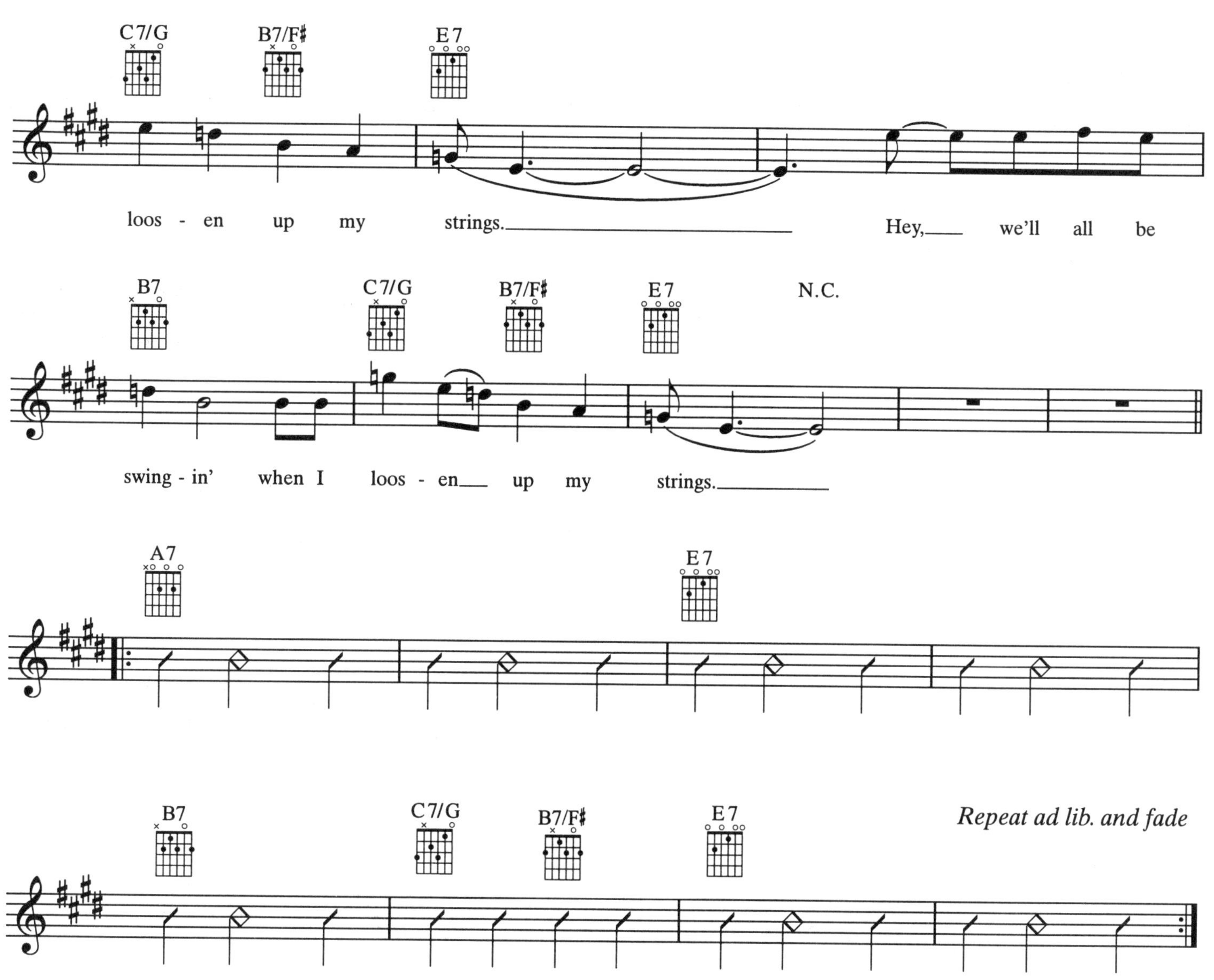

Verse 2:
Every night when the sun goes down,
You won't find me hangin' around.
I'm in locomotion like a rock out on a roll.
I'm nobody's puppet. I'm out of control.
(To Chorus:)

MERCURY BLUES

Written by
ROBERT GEDDINGS and K.C. DOUGLAS

Mercury Blues - 2 - 1
GFM0009

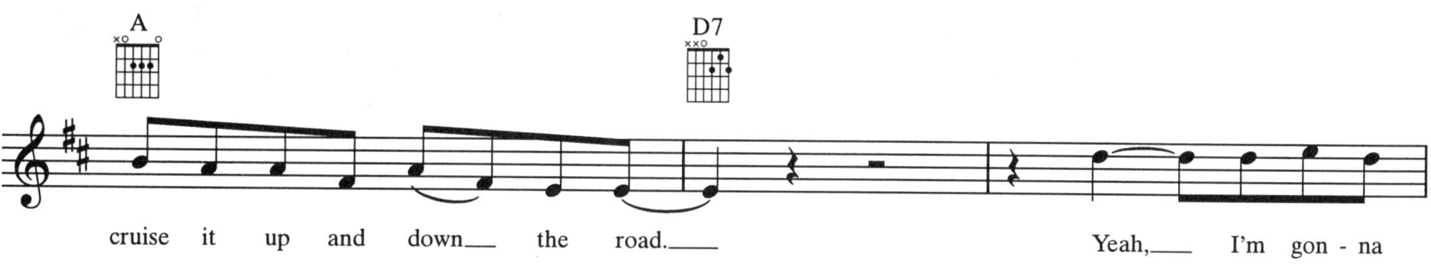

Verse 2:
Well, the girl I love,
I stole her from a friend.
He got lucky, stole her back again.
She heard he had a Mercury.
Lord, she's crazy 'bout a Mercury.
I'm gonna buy me a Mercury
And cruise it up and down the road.

Verse 3:
Well, hey now, mama,
You look so fine
Ridin' 'round in your Mercury '49.
Crazy 'bout a Mercury.
Lord, I'm crazy 'bout a Mercury.
I'm gonna buy me a Mercury
And cruise it up and down the road.

Verse 4:
Well, my baby went out,
She didn't stay long.
Bought herself a Mercury, come a cruisin' home.
She's crazy 'bout a Mercury.
Yeah, she's crazy 'bout a Mercury.
I'm gonna buy me a Mercury
And cruise it up and down the road.

NEVER KNEW LONELY

Words and Music by
VINCE GILL

Verse 2:
You are my rock and the strength I need
To keep me sane in this life that I lead.
Now I'm not with you and my broken heart bleeds;
I never knew lonely till you.
(To Chorus:)

Verse 3:
Instrumental ad lib.

Verse 4:
I can't make up for the times I've been gone,
But I'll prove I love you in the words of this song.
Back in your arms, girl, it's where I belong;
I never knew lonley till you.
(To Chorus:)

POOR, POOR PITIFUL ME

Words and Music by
WARREN ZEVON

Capo at 4th fret

Poor, Poor Pitiful Me - 3 - 1
GFM0009

D/A
A
E/A
A
D/A
A
D/A
A
me.
Verse 2:
Well, I met a man out in Hol - ly - wood and
I ain't nam - in' names.
But he real - ly worked me
o - ver good, just like Jes - se James.
Yes, he
D
A
real - ly worked me o - ver good, he was a cred - it to his gen - der.
D
A
He put me through some chang - es, Lord, sort - a
Chorus:
like a War - ing blend - er.
D
A
E
A
Poor, poor pit - i - ful me!
D
A
Poor, poor pit - i - ful me!
D
A
E
A
Oh, these boys won't let me be.

Verse 3:
Well, I met a boy in the Vieux-Carres,
Down in Yokohama.
He picked me up and he threw me down,
Sayin', "Please don't hurt me, mama."
(To Chorus:)

THE RIVER

Words and Music by
VICTORIA SHAW and GARTH BROOKS

G
D
G/D
D
if I nev - er try. So I will sail my ves - sel till the
A
1.
D
riv - er runs dry.
2. Too man - y
2.
D
A/C♯
Bridge:
Bm
G
And there's bound to be rough wa - ters and I
D
D/F♯
G
Em7
D/F♯
know I'll take some falls, but with the Good Lord as my cap - tain, I can
G
Asus
make it through them all. Yes, I will
Chorus:
E
A/E
E
A/E
E
sail my ves - sel till the riv - er runs dry. Like a
A
E/G♯
F♯m7
B
C♯m
B/D♯
bird up - on the wind, these wa - ters are my sky. I'll nev - er

Verse 2:
Too many times we stand aside
And let the waters slip away
Till what we put off till tomorrow
Has now become today.
So don't you sit upon the shoreline
And say you're satisfied.
Choose to chance the rapids
And dare to dance the tide. Yes, I will . . .
(To Chorus:)

SHE'S GONNA MAKE IT

Words and Music by
KENT BLAZY, KIM WILLIAMS
and GARTH BROOKS

She's Gonna Make It - 2 - 1
GFM0009

Verse 2:
And you know it's not like she's forgot about him,
She's just dealing with the pain.
And the fact that she's survived so well without him,
You know it's driving him insane.
And the crazy thing about it is,
She'd take him back,
But the fool in him that walked out
Is the fool that just won't ask.
(To Chorus:)

SOMEONE YOU USED TO KNOW

Words and Music by
TIM JOHNSON and RORY LEE

Verse 2:
Bet you didn't tell him
'Bout those weekends at the coast,
Or how we used to argue
'Bout who loved who the most.
Well, I guess I won that one,
'Cause I still need you so,
But to you, I'm just
Someone you used to know.
(To Chorus:)

SOMETHING THAT WE DO

Words and Music by
CLINT BLACK and SKIP EWING

Am7
be, though we can find our strength and in - spi - ra - tion
G C
in - de - pen - dent - ly. The way we work to - geth -
G/B
- er is what sets our love a - part, so close -
B♭ To Coda Am7 D
- ly that we can't tell where I end and where you start. It
rit.
Verse 3:
G D/G C (9)
gives me heart, re - mem - b'ring how we start - ed with a sim -
a tempo
G C (9) G
- ple vow. There's so much to look back on now.
Am7 D G
Still it feels brand new. We're on a road that has
D/G C G
no end, and each day we be - gin a - gain. Love's

C
G
Am7
D7sus
not just some - thing that___ we're in, it's some - thing that___ we do.___
G
D/G
C
G
D.S. 𝄋 al Coda
C
G
Am7
D7sus
G
G/B
Coda
Am7
D
G
end and where___ you start. Love is wide,___
rit.
a tempo
D/G
C/G
G
love is long, love is deep___ and love___ is strong.
C/G
G
Love is why___ I love___ this song,___
Am7
D
G
I hope you love it, too.___ I re - mem - ber well___ the day___
D
C
G
___ we wed,___ I can see that pic - ture in___ my head.___ Love

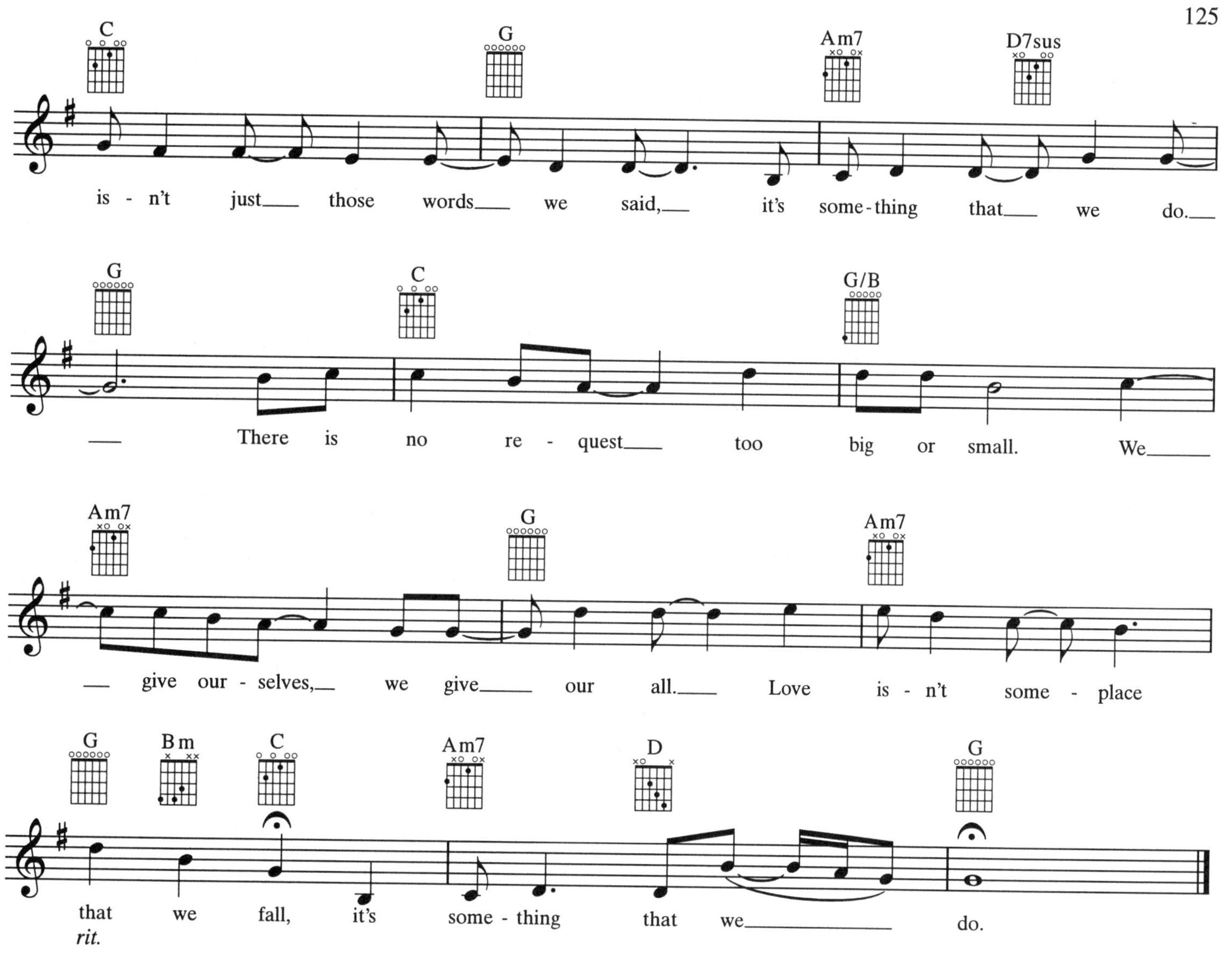

Verse 2:
It's holding tight, lettin' go,
It's flyin' high and layin' low.
Let your strongest feelings show
And your weakness, too.
It's a little and a lot to ask,
An endless and a welcome task.
Love isn't something that we have,
It's something that we do.
(To Bridge:)

THAT DON'T IMPRESS ME MUCH

Words and Music by
SHANIA TWAIN and R.J. LANGE

That Don't Impress Me Much - 3 - 1
GFM0009

Chorus:
F C G Am F C
press me much. So you got the { brain,__ looks,__ moves,__ } but have you
G Am F C G Am
got the touch?__ Now don't get me wrong,__ yeah, I think you're al - right, but
F C To Coda G
that won't keep me warm in the mid - dle of the night.
1.
N.C. Am F C G Am F C G
That don't im - press__ me much.
2. I
2.
N.C. Am F C G Am F
That don't im - press__ me much. (Inst. solo ad lib....
D.S. al Coda
C G Am F C G Am F C G
... end solo) 3. You're
Coda G
Chorus:
F C G
- dle of the night. That don't im - press me much.

Verse 2:
I never knew a guy who carried a mirror in his pocket
And a comb up his sleeve, just in case.
And all that extra hold gel in your hair oughta a lock it,
'Cause heaven forbid it should fall outta place.
Oh, oh, you think you're special.
Oh, oh, you think you're something else.
(Spoken:) OK, so you're Brad Pitt.
(To Chorus:)

Verse 3:
You're one of those guys who likes to shine his machine.
You make me take off my shoes before you let me get in.
I can't believe you kiss your car good-night.
Come on, baby, tell me, you must be jokin', right?
Oh, oh, you think you're something special.
Oh, oh, you think you're something else.
(Spoken:) OK, so you've got a car.
(To Chorus:)

TWO TEARDROPS

2.3.
B♭
G/B
Csus
C
me a ride to the sea."
Oh, the o-
Chorus:
Dm7
Am7
B♭
cean's a lit - tle bit big - ger to - night, two more tear - drops
2. See additional lyrics
F
Dm7
Am7
some - bod - y cried. One of them hap - py and one of them blu - er than
B♭
Csus
Dm7
blue. The tide goes out and the tide
Am7
B♭
F
C/E
comes in. And some - day they'll be tear - drops a - gain, re -
Dm7
Am7
B♭
leased in a mo - ment of plea - sure or a mo - ment of pain.
Am7
Gm7
F/A
Gm7/C
Then they drift on down and ride to the sea a - gain.

Verse 2:
The other tear said, "We've got a connection.
I'm a tear of sorrow, born of rejection.
I'm from the sad, brown eyes of her old flame.
She told him they would be life-long companions,
Left him with questions and not any answers.
I was on his cheek as he stood there calling her name.
I could tell he had a lot of my friends for company.
So I drifted on down and caught me a ride to the sea."
(To Chorus:)

Verse 3:
Last night I sat in the waiting room.
The nurse walked in and gave me the news;
It's a baby girl and they're both fine.
An old man sittin' not ten feet away
Just lost his wife, and he said to me,
"You've got a brand-new angel and I've lost mine.
I guess the good Lord giveth and the good Lord taketh away."

Chorus 2:
Oh, the ocean's a little bit bigger tonight,
Two more teardrops somebody cried.
One of them happy and one of them bluer than blue.
The tide goes out and the tide comes in.
A whole new circle of life begins
Where tears are a part of the pleasure and part of the pain,
Till they drift on down and ride to the sea again.

THIS KISS

Words and Music by
ROBIN LERNER, ANNIE ROBOFF
and BETH NIELSEN CHAPMAN

D/F♯ G C Am7
roof - top, un - der the sky, oh. You can kiss me with the win - dows o - pen while the
D/F♯ G G/B C G/B Am7 G
rain comes blow - in' in - side, oh. Kiss me in sweet, slow mo - tion.
D/F♯ G F♯m7 F♯m7/B
Let's let ev - 'ry - thing slide. You got me float - ing, you got me fly - ing.
F♯ F♯/A♯ B C♯
It's the way you love me. It's a feel - ing like this.
F♯ F♯/A♯ B C♯ F♯ F♯/A♯
It's cen - trif - u - gal mo - tion. It's per - pet - u - al bliss. It's that piv - ot - al mo - ment.
B C♯ F♯ F♯/A♯ B D♯m7 C♯
It's, ah, sub - lim - i - nal. This kiss, this kiss. It's crim - i - nal.
F♯ F♯/A♯ B D♯m7 C♯ F♯ F♯/A♯
This kiss, this kiss. It's the way you love me,
Repeat and fade
B D♯m7 C♯ F♯ F♯/A♯ B D♯m7 C♯
ba - by. It's the way you love me, dar - ling.

WHAT IF JESUS COMES BACK LIKE THAT

Words and Music by
PAT BUNCH and DOUG JOHNSON

What If Jesus Comes Back Like That - 2 - 1
GFM0009

Verse 2:
Born with a habit of drug abuse,
She couldn't help what her mama used.
It wasn't like she got to choose,
Now she's lyin' there all alone.
Got a monkey on her back,
Nurses say they never saw a smile like that.
Doctor says she might stand a chance,
If somebody takes her home.

Chorus 2:
What if Jesus comes back like that,
Two months early and hooked on crack?
Will we let him in or turn our back?
What if Jesus comes back like that?
Oh, what if Jesus comes back like that?
(To Bridge:)

Chorus 3:
What if Jesus comes back like that?
Will he cry when he sees where our hearts are at?
Will he let us in or turn his back?
What if Jesus comes back like that?
Hey, what if Jesus comes back like that?

WHAT THE COWGIRLS DO

What the Cowgirls Do - 2 - 1
GFM0009

Verse 2:
They ain't no different up in Oklahoma,
They ain't afraid to stay up till dawn.
They love to cut a rug and chug-a-lug
Longnecks till their money's all gone.
(To Chorus:)

Verse 3:
Instrumental ad lib.
(To Chorus:)

Verse 4:
There's cowgirls all across the country,
From Baton Rouge to Bangor, Maine.
It ain't hard to see they'll be the death of me,
They gonna drive my little heart insane.
(To Chorus:)

WHERE THE GREEN GRASS GROWS

Words and Music by
CRAIG WISEMAN and JESS LEARY

Where the Green Grass Grows - 2 - 1
GFM0009

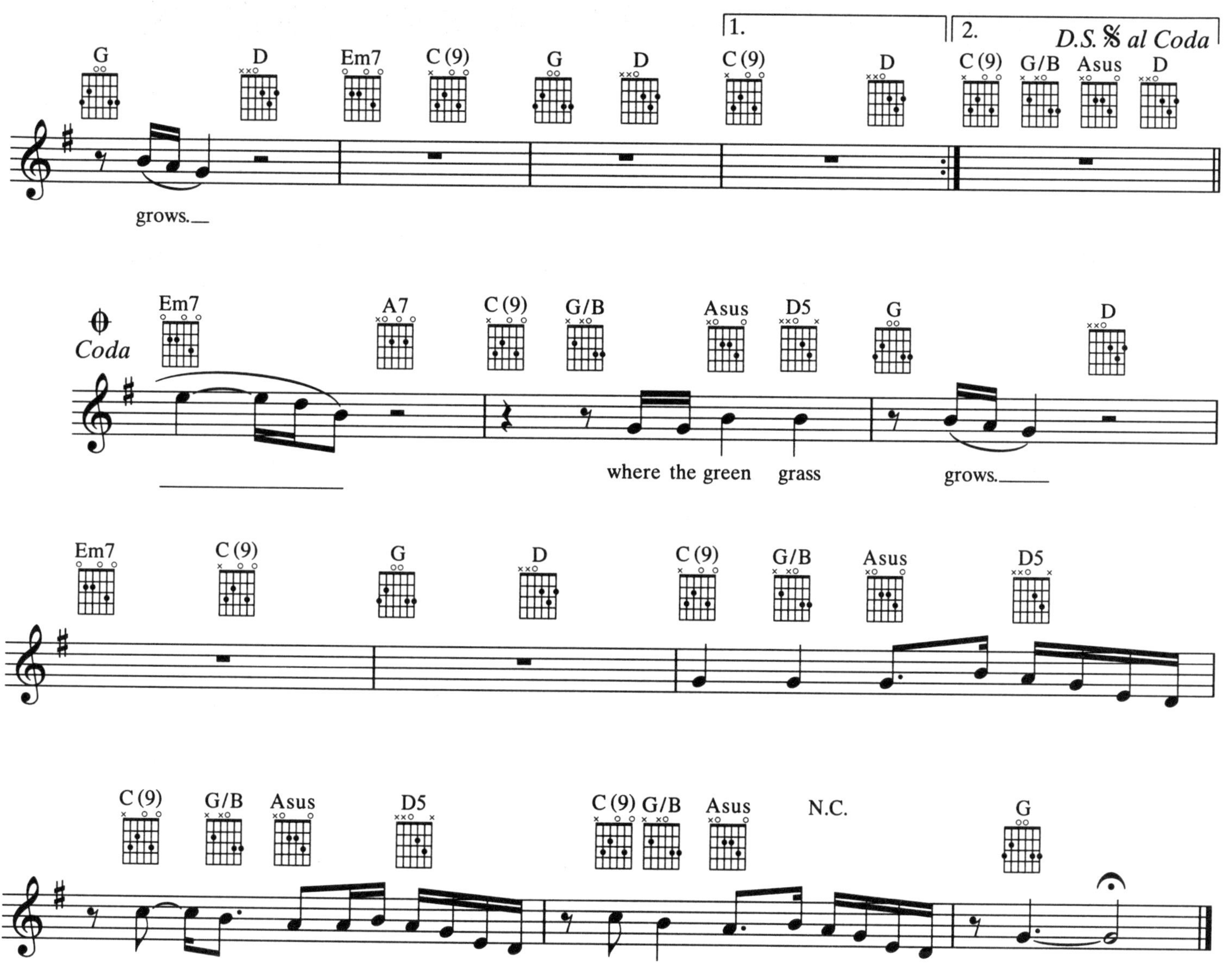

Verse 2:
I'm from a map dot,
A stop sign on a blacktop.
I caught the first bus I could hop from there.
But all of this glitter is getting dark,
There's concrete growing in the city park.
I don't know who my neighbors are,
There's bars on the corners and bars on my heart.
But. . .
(To Chorus:)

WRONG NIGHT

Words and Music by
JOSH LEO and RICK BOWLES

A
D
cross the sky. Is it grav - i - ty or des - ti - ny?
A
Ei - ther way, there is noth - ing I can do. Looks like I picked the
To Coda
1.
E7
D N.C.
A
wrong night not to fall in love with you.
E
D
A
2. I brief -
2.
D
A
N.C.
to fall in love with you.
G
D
D.S. al Coda
F
G
A
Sud-den-ly I heard

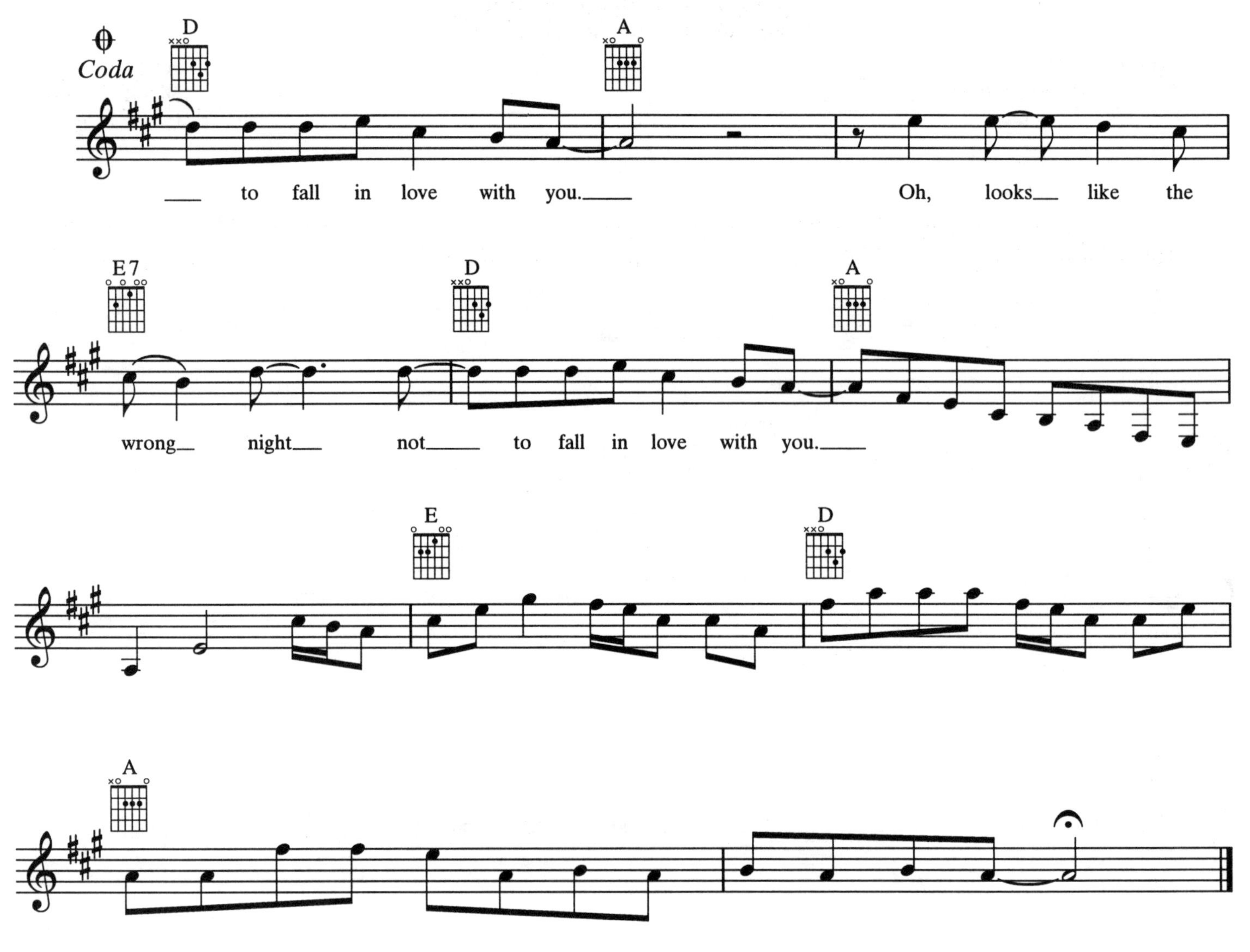

Verse 2:
I briefly resisted, but my heart insisted
It was gonna be giving in.
Hard as I was trying, there was no denying
Which one of us would win.
You came up beside me and asked if I'd be
Wantin' to have a dance.
Right then I knew this thing was out of my hands.
(To Chorus:)

YOU MOVE ME

Capo at 2nd fret
Moderately slow ♩ = 88
Verse:
Words and Music by
GORDON KENNEDY and
PIERCE PETTIS
D F♯m D
1. This is how it seems to me, life is on - ly ther - a - py,
2. See additional lyrics
F♯m G D A
real ex - pen - sive and no guar - an - tees.
D F♯m D
And so I lie here on the couch with my heart hang - ing out,
F♯m G D
fro - zen sol - id with fear, like a rock in the
Chorus:
A Asus A Bm G
ground. Oh, but you move me.
D F♯m Bm G D A
You give me cour - age I didn't know I had. You move
Bm G D F♯m Bm G
me. Now I can't go with you and
D A
1.
G2
stay where I am, so you move me.
You Move Me - 3 - 1
GFM0009

2.
G2
move me.
Bridge:
Em
G
D
You go whis - tling in the dark, mak - ing light of it
A
F♯m
Em
mak - ing light of it and I fol - low with my
G
A
Asus
A
heart, laugh - ing all the way. Oh, 'cause you move
Chorus:
Bm
G
D
F♯m
Bm
G
me. You get me danc - ing and
D
A
Bm
G
D
F♯m
you make me sing. You move me. Now I'm
Bm
G
D
A
G2
tak - ing de - light in ev - 'ry lit - tle thing, how you move me.
D
A
Em
D
A
Oh, you move me. Oh, you move

Verse 2:
This is how love was to me,
I could look and not see.
Going through the emotions,
Not knowing what they mean.
And it scared me so much
That I just wouldn't budge.
I might have stayed there forever,
If not for your touch.

Chorus 2:
Oh, but you move me
Out of myself and into the fire.
You move me.
Now I'm burning with love
And with hope and desire.
You move me.
(To Bridge:)

YOU BETTER THINK TWICE

Words and Music by
VINCE GILL and REED NIELSEN

Repeat ad lib. and fade

Verse 2:
You really must think I'm something,
Talkin' trash about my best friend.
I just hate to see you wind up with nothing,
'Cause you're way too good for him.
I know that you don't believe me,
But I've been with him when he's runnin' 'round.
He don't mean to hurt nobody,
He ain't never gonna settle down.
(To Chorus:)

Verse 3:
Instrumental
(To Chorus:)

YOU'RE STILL THE ONE

Verse 2:
Ain't nothin' better,
We beat the odds together.
I'm glad we didn't listen.
Look at what we would be missin'.
They said, "I bet they'll never make it."
But just look at us holdin' on.
We're together, still goin' strong.
(To Chorus:)

YOU'RE EASY ON THE EYES

Chorus:
A7
A
... end solo) } You're eas - y on the eyes,
hard on the heart.
You look so
E
D
A
good, but the way things look ain't the way they are.
D
Bet - ter say good - bye
be - fore this goes too
E
D
To Coda
far,
'cause now I re - al - ize, you're eas - y on the
1.
E
A7
D/A
eyes, hard on the heart.
A7
D/A
2.
E
D.S. al Coda
2. I
eyes, hard on the heart.

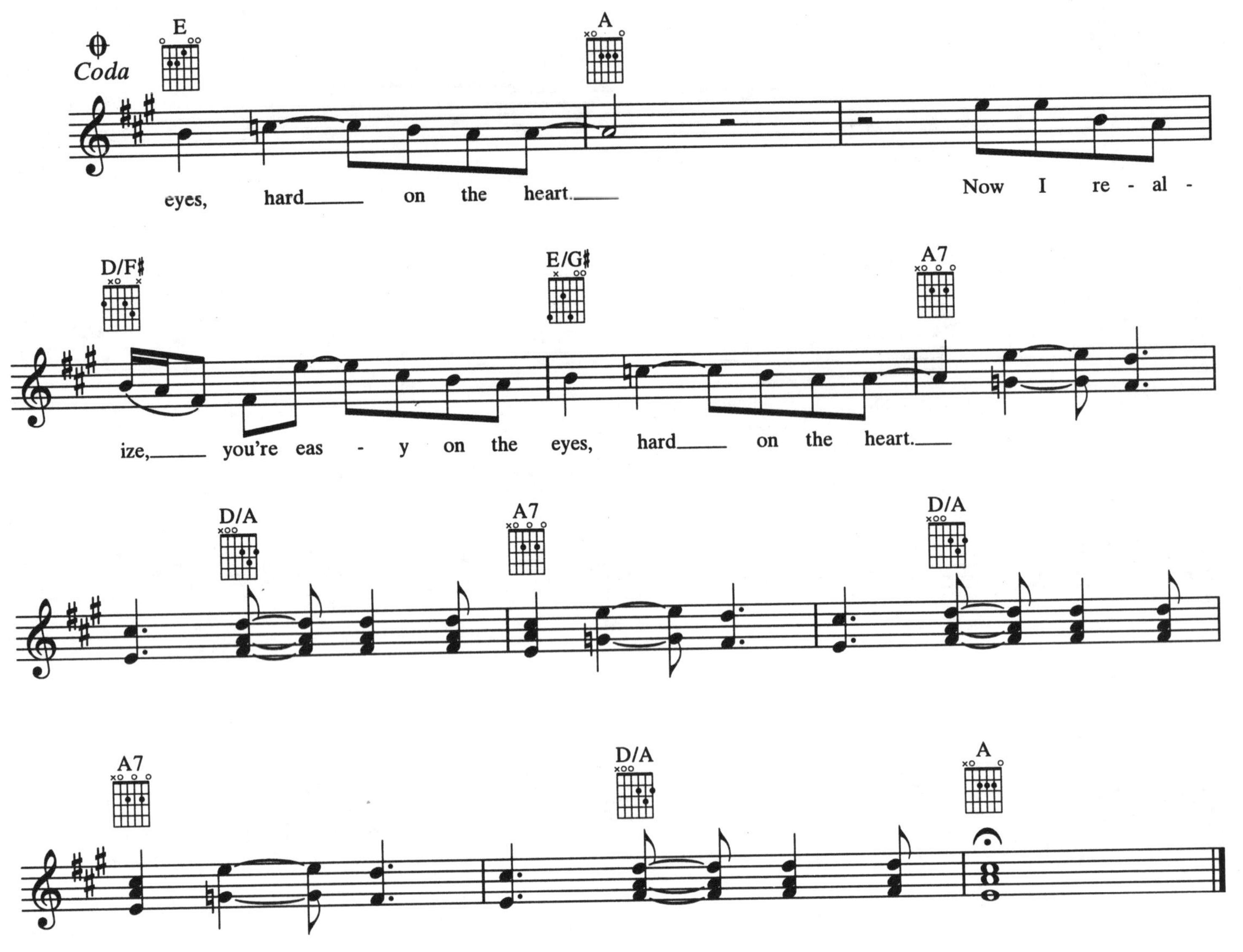

Verse 2:
I got to admit, you got a smile
That really reeled me in for a while.
But it ain't funny, honey, what you put me through.
So why don't you send me your photograph?
It'd hurt a lot less than taking you back.
Then I could still have my favorite part of you.
(To Chorus:)